GETTING ON THE INFORMATION SUPERHIGHWAY

Wally Bock

CRISP PUBLICATIONS, INC.
Menlo Park, California

GETTING ON THE INFORMATION SUPERHIGHWAY

Wally Bock

CREDITS
Managing Editor: **Kathleen Barcos**
Editor: **Carol Henry**
Designer: **ExecuStaff**
Typesetting: **ExecuStaff**
Cover Design: **Kathleen Palmer**

Copyright © 1996 by Crisp Publications, Inc.
Printed in the United States of America by Bawden Printing Company.

Library of Congress Catalog Card Number 95-68991
Bock, Wally
Getting on the Information Superhighway
ISBN 1-56052-327-1

PREFACE

If you're like most of the rest of us, you've seen book after book and article after article about the Information Superhighway. You've noticed the magazine covers about the Internet, and caught the television specials about the denizens of the online world.

But maybe you don't quite know what all the fuss is about. After all, you're not a techie, you're just an ordinary person. Does the online world have anything that you need? And how will you ever find the time and money you need to learn about it? Or maybe you think you *should* get online, but you're not sure exactly where to start. What do you need? What should you do first? Second?

If this sounds like you, then hang on. If you're an intelligent person who's a bit puzzled or confused by all the Internet and online hype, this book is for you.

This book is about why normal folks like you and me should be online. OK, We hear you asking, why? There are only three reasons to go online: people, information and business. When you go online, you can manage and communicate with any or all of those—faster, easier and more effectively than you can otherwise. Examples? Here goes.

> Bert's a traveling businessperson whose job takes him on the road a lot. His wife's a professional with her own active life and travel schedule. And their kids are in high school and colleges around the country. Bert and his family use electronic mail (e-mail) to stay in touch with one another because they find it cheaper and better than long-distance telephone. And sometimes they all get online together for a little family meeting. That's some-thing they couldn't do at all without being online.

Jane's a salesperson. She's discovered that she's far more effective if she can find out a lot about a prospect before she makes the first face-to-face call. She uses databases and friends—all online—to get the scoop before she shows up. That way she knows about her prospective customer and the prospect's industry, so she can do a better job of matching her company's products with the customer's needs. It couldn't happen as efficiently without being online.

Tom, Martha, Phyllis, and Dave all work for the same company but in different locations. Because they're all online, they can be assigned to an electronic project team that can do most of its work without the hassle and expense of face-to-face meetings. They get more done. And, according to the latest research, they also make better decisions because they're online.

Steve's hobby is collecting antique guitars. There's not a single other person in his county that shares his passion. But around the world, there are thousands of folks online who do. He communicates with them regularly, discussing facts, finds and fantasies about something they all love.

Ray's a single parent who can't always be around when his child, Ginny, is doing homework. Getting his family online has solved this problem. Now Ginny can get help with her homework when she needs it, and get it from experts. Ray often leaves e-mail for his daughter, reminding her about assignments and chores, telling her he loves her and letting her know when he'll be home if his plans change.

That's just a sample. All these people and millions more have discovered that their lives are better, richer and more productive because they're online. You can have the same advantages. But you have to experience being online to really understand what's different about it and how it can change your life. Remember when word processing and computer spreadsheets were first introduced? Until you saw them work, you probably didn't understand what they could do for you.

When you first heard about word processing, you probably said something like, "Why do I need that? I've got a typewriter." It wasn't until you had your first opportunity to move a whole paragraph to a new page, or change part of a long document without retyping the whole thing that you saw the benefits of the word processing program. Or what about the first time someone told you about a spreadsheet program? If you were like most of us, you thought you could already do your accounting just as well with a pencil, a calculator and a big sheet of ledger paper. Then maybe you watched someone change just one number—and all the other related numbers changed automatically. For lots of folks, just the spreadsheet program was reason enough to rush out and buy a computer.

Likewise, to understand what's going on in the online world, you must experience it. You should start slowly and painlessly, building your knowledge and experience in small steps. This book will help you do that. Here's how it will work.

▶ We'll start by introducing you to the online world and its jargon. There's always jargon in any new field, and we'll tell you what it is.

▶ Next we'll explain, in simple, nontechnical terms, what kind of equipment (hardware and software) you need to get started.

▶ After that, we'll give you a step-by-step procedure for getting connected. We'll help you pick the online service that's best for you to start with and lay out your first five sessions. You'll know exactly what to do every step of the way. Even if you stop there, you'll have made the online world a part of your life and you'll reap significant benefits.

▶ Once you've mastered the basics, we'll give you the information you need to explore this magical world. There's enough here about services and features to keep you busy exploring for months if you choose. Or you can jump to a specific subject only when you need to know about it, or to do something new.

▶ And finally, we'll help you figure out where to go next. The online world is changing fast, but you can handle it once you have the basics.

Now it's time to get started. Turn to the next section, and do it now. Don't wait for a better time. There's no time like the present—and the sooner you get started, the sooner all the benefits of being online will be yours.

CONTENTS

I
GETTING
READY

THE BASICS

Definitions

Let's begin with some basic definitions.

When we use the term *online,* we mean "connected to another computer through a phone line." An *online service* is one that provides information and other features via that connection.

The computer at the other end (the *remote computer*) may be a big computer like the one at the America Online headquarters in Vienna, Virginia. Or it may be a PC or Mac on a local *bulletin board system (BBS)*. Your own computer may be at work or at home. When two computers are connected via a phone line, then they (and you, if you're working one of them) are online.

A *computer bulletin board* (BBS) is like the cork bulletin board in the office, or down at the supermarket, or at the community center. It's a computer where people "post" messages and sometimes ads.

Major *general purpose gateways* are services such as America Online, CompuServe, Delphi and GEnie. They offer a broad array of services to their subscribers including e-mail, reference, conferencing groups and more. We'll spend most of our time in this book talking about them, because they're the route most people take to get connected.

Special purpose gateways are services such as Dialog, Dow Jones News Retrieval, DataTimes and others. They provide specific services, usually reference and news.

Then there's *the Internet.* The Internet is a network of computer networks, and it links millions of people around the world. The Internet is a way to send e-mail from one service to another. It has special services like Usenet; a collection of *newsgroups* (actually, they're more like discussion groups); archives of data files; and places to do business. The Internet lets you connect to more resources than any system, but it's also the hardest to use. We won't spend much time on the Internet in this book.

What You Can Do Online

Now the real question: *Why should you be interested in this stuff?*

Probably the best way to illustrate what you can do online is to give you a list. Take a look at the following list of "Things You Can Do Online." As you review the list, put a check mark next to the things you already do in the physical world. Circle those things you might want to do online if you knew how. Your list might look something like this:

Things You Can Do Online

❑ E-mail to clients.

❑ Stay in touch with a collaborator.

❑ Sell articles.

❑ Send a news release.

❑ Make reservations.

❑ Be interviewed.

❑ Conduct an interview.

❑ Send an article.

❑ Send a file.

❑ Talk with friends.

❑ Get known.

❑ Hold a conference.

❑ Find the largest manufacturer in Denver.

❑ Identify the president of that company.

❑ Find prospects.

❑ Research a prospect.

❑ Pay taxes.

❑ Pay bills.

❑ Do market research.

❑ Research a topic.

❑ Figure out the coming hot topics.

❑ Have a client contact you.

❑ Find stories about a client.

❑ Get a credit report on a prospect.

❑ Run a committee.

❑ Have a mastermind group.

❑ Read a newspaper.

❑ Read a magazine.

❑ Stay in touch with your office

❑ Play a game.

❑ Make a friend.

❑ Send mail internationally.

❑ Send files internationally.

❑ Keep up on trends.

❑ Get a phone number.

❑ Make a donation to charity.

❑ Enter a contest.

❑ Discuss trivia.

❑ Write to the president.

❑ Attend a support group.

❑ Sell a product.

❑ Negotiate a contract.

❑ Provide a service.

❑ Advertise.

❑ Have a brainstorming session.

Advantages of Going Online

OK, that makes a neat list. But why do them online? What's the advantage?

▶ **You do things online because you can do them faster that way.** An electronic mail (e-mail) letter arrives seconds after you send it. You can get information right away when you need it. A transfer of funds from one bank account to another is done as soon as you are.

▶ **You do things online because you can reach more people that way.** In the physical world you're limited by the folks you know, or whose phone number or address you have. When you're online, you can reach thousands of people that you wouldn't know otherwise. And you can do it at any time of the day or night. These people can be in a variety of places around the globe, some of which you need a passport to travel to.

▶ **You do things online because you can do more with what you get.** When you get information from an online source, it's already in your computer. If you want to quote from it in a report or other document, all you have to do is copy and paste. If you want to search the data for a keyword, you can have your computer do that for you. If you want to send information to someone else, you can do that at the touch of a key.

We can break all of this down into three general categories: You go online because you want to reach people, get information, or do business more effectively than you can otherwise. To help you figure out how this might work for you, we've provided three worksheets. There's one for people, one for information, and one for business. Each worksheet is divided into two columns.

The left-hand column is for those things or folks or activities that are already important to you. When we move on to choosing services and deciding how you can best use online services, you'll need to use this list.

The right-hand column is for those things or people or activities that you'd like to connect with or find out about or use, but that aren't part of your current world. You might list a strictly online activity here, such as "pay bills by computer" on the business worksheet. Or you might list a person you'd like to contact but can't reach by traditional methods. As we move on, you'll see how you can do these things online.

Once you've got an idea of what you might want to do online, we'll set about getting you connected.

People Who Are Already Important	People I'd Like to Connect With

Kinds of Information That Are Important Now	Kinds of Information I'd Like to Have

Business I Do Now That Might Work Online	Business I'd Like to Try Online

WHAT KINDS OF SERVICES ARE AVAILABLE?

In the last section you got an idea of why you should be online. You found out the kinds of things you *can* do, and identified some of the things you might *want* to do. In this section, you will

- Find out about what services are available to you

- Pick a service to start with that's right for you

- Develop the strategy you'll use for entering this new world

Learning to get connected and to get the most from the online world is a lot like learning to cook or ride a bike. You won't learn it just by reading about it. And you'll find that some things will come easy to you, while others will be tougher.

One thing that *won't* be different in learning about connecting to the online world is that it's best to start with the easy things and move on to the more difficult things. That's the kind of strategy we'll outline later in this section.

And, like bike riding or cooking, some people want to go further than others. Some want to ride a bike so they can have fun cruising around the neighborhood. Others want some serious transportation; they'll use their bike to go shopping and for local trips. Finally, there are some who want to ride their bikes in competition. They enter races and take long, cross-country rides.

The online world is like that, too. You may be interested only in connecting for fun and games. Or you may put your online connections to serious business use. You may even find that you want to mine every single resource out there and become a real "Net surfer." You don't have to decide right now which of those places you'll wind up. Right now let's concentrate on fundamentals, starting with what's available.

Types of Online Services

There are four basic kinds of online services, mentioned briefly in the last section. Now we're going to see what your options are with each kind of service. Look at the following chart to see how they compare. You'll also find a detailed listing of services in the Appendices, along with contact numbers.

Type of Service	Examples	Characteristics
General Purpose Gateways	• Prodigy • CompuServe • America Online • eWorld • GEnie • Delphi • Microsoft Network	• Broad range of services • Connection to other services including the Internet • Often provide their own software • Large numbers of subscribers
Special Purpose Gateways	• Dow Jones News Retrieval • DataTimes • DIALOG • Association Bulletin Boards • Recruitment Services	• Special focus such as topic, information source, industry, function
Bulletin Boards	• The WELL • Cyberia • Association Bulletin Boards	• Local or special interest • Newspapers run these a lot
Internet Services	• NetCom • Pipeline • Local Internet Providers	• Range from easy connections to those requiring special hardware and software • Even easy connections require you to be "online knowledgeable"

General purpose gateways include the major online services, such as Prodigy, CompuServe, and America Online. They offer a broad range of services, as well as serving as gateways to other services.

Special purpose gateways have a special focus. One such service is the Dow Jones News Retrieval. It's set up to provide comprehensive financial news to subscribers. Another is DataTimes, which offers the text of newspapers from around the country. NewsNet specializes in very narrowly focused industry newsletters and specialty news sources from around the world.

Somewhere between the two types of gateways lie **bulletin board services** (BBSs). They, as well, often provide a way for subscribers to get to other services; that makes them a lot like general purpose gateways. But a BBS usually has some special focus. There are bulletin boards with a geographical emphasis, for example—such as the Virtual Weekend BBS in Columbia, Missouri. Some bulletin boards focus on a special industry or interest. One of these is the Human Resources Information Service. This industry bulletin board provides information files and connections that are of interest to human resources professionals. In fact, some associations have access to this bulletin board as a benefit of membership.

Yet another type of online service is defined by the kind of people it attracts. **The WELL** (Whole Earth 'Lectronic Link) in the San Francisco Bay Area, for instance, attracts a group of users who are mostly urban and interested in intellectual discussion. Though a majority of the WELL's participants are from the Bay Area, many dial in from all over the world to enjoy the intellectual stimulation the service offers.

The Internet is the "mother of all networks" for a couple of reasons. First, it links most of the existing services into a giant connection network. Second, because it links all kinds of services, it has the broadest array of resources available.

Why not just use the Internet, then? Why even bother with other sources? There are a couple of reasons. Let's return to our analogy of riding a bike. Some bikes—such as tricycles or mountain bikes—are best for a specific kind of riding. That's true for online services, too. If you want a specialized newsletter, then NewsNet will be more effective than anything else. If you want to use only one online service, then one of the general gateways will probably suffice. Interested in your local sports team, or news of your profession or industry? Then you may find a bulletin board is your best bet.

If you're reading this book to find out about getting online, then you need to consider ease of use, as well. Most people learn to ride on a fairly simple bike, and then move on to more complex equipment if they have the need and desire. The fact is, some services are a whole lot harder to use than others. And the Internet is probably the hardest of all.

There are several ways to get to the Internet, however. You could call them different kinds of bikes. Recently the popular general purpose gateways—CompuServe, Prodigy and America Online—have started adding Internet access as part of their services. These will be an excellent way for you to get to the Internet, meet most of your early needs, and let you figure out what all the fuss is about. Later you can look at more demanding ways to connect.

There are also several services (two of them are Netcom and Pipeline) that make getting connected to the Internet easier than it used to be. They're still a bit more difficult to use than the general purpose gateways, but they may be a solution for you if you want more than those gateways provide.

Acquiring Your Skills

In bike riding there are three things that go into determining whether you're going to be able to do a particular level of activity well: equipment (what kind of bike you have), fitness (how physically ready you are for the challenge), and experience (whether you're knowledgeable about tricks of the trade). The same is true on the Information Superhighway.

You have to have the **equipment** necessary to contact the service you want. Equipment refers to your computer, or hardware, your software, and your telephone connection. We'll discuss these elements more in a later section.

You have to be **fit enough** for the task you want to perform. Online, fitness for a particular service or activity consists of "technological tolerance" and the way you approach change. If you're comfortable with technology and if you like learning new tasks, then you will probably push ahead a little faster when you're working online. If you approach change slowly and cautiously, or if technology makes you a little nervous, then you should move a bit more slowly.

And you need **experience.** This includes experience with the online services, with similar computer activities and with computers in general. If you're already familiar with computers and a good number of programs (applications), you'll have an easier time getting online than if you are new to the world of computers and have only used a couple of programs.

Fitness and experience often go together. If you've had to learn lots of computer programs, for example, you're more likely to be comfortable learning new but similar tasks to get online. In other words, your experience will increase your fitness.

How does all this relate to the online services we've talked about? Take a look at the chart on page 15.

Here's a bit of explanation. You'll see that the general purpose gateways require a level of fitness and hardware that is usually lower than what's needed for using the special purpose gateways or the Internet. We've listed some specific services on the chart to give you an idea of where they fall.

Way out on the right edge of the chart, requiring the greatest level of equipment and experience is full connection to the Internet. That's because such a connection requires you to be very comfortable with using online services and also invest in special software and a telephone connection. That's a lot for most folks.

Look at the services listed in the medium range, though. There we've listed Netcom and Pipeline, two of the services that will let you connect to the Internet without special equipment. They also have a graphical interface, so you'll find them fairly easy to use.

The reason these services aren't in the low-experience part of the chart is that they do assume you're already familiar with the online basics we'll be covering in this book. You'll pretty much have to figure out how to use these services on your own, without the help of manuals and easily available support lines.

We've placed bulletin boards in the medium range, but this will vary a lot by bulletin board. Some of them are very easy to use.

That's the range of services that are out there. Let's move on now and figure out what service is right for you to get started.

Service	Prodigy	America Online	Compuserve	GEnie	Dow Jones News Ret.	Many BBS	Dialog	DataTimes	Internet (Full Connection)
		eWorld Microsoft Network		Delphi Netcom Pipeline	NewsNet	WELL			
Hardware	Most computers Mac or Windows systems easier. Modem	Most computers Mac or Windows systems easier. Modem	Most computers Mac or Windows systems easier. Modem	Most computers Mac or Windows systems easier.	Most computers Mac or Windows systems easier.	Most computers Mac or Windows systems easier.	Most computers Mac or Windows systems easier.	Most computers Mac or Windows systems easier.	Special telephone connection required.
				Because you will be downloading and transferring lots of files, a high speed modem is more important from here on.					
Software	These services provide their own MAC and/or Windows software. They also provide their own connection to the Internet and World Wide Web		Automating software is desirable.	From here on you will need general purpose communications software such as Crosstalk, Procomm, Red Rider, Versaterm, or White Knight to access services and bulletin boards.					Special software required
Fitness or Experience Level	Lowest	Lowest	Low	Medium	Medium	Medium	High	High	High

WHICH SERVICE SHOULD YOU START WITH?

In this section we're going to help you decide which service is the one you should try first.

The principle is that you want to start with something that's going to be as easy as possible while still being productive. And that in turn means starting with one of the services with the lowest need for fitness or experience. That would be Prodigy, America Online, eWorld, or the new Microsoft Network.

Start there even if you already have a high level of fitness and experience. If you haven't been online yet, you'll want to get accustomed to the online world in the easiest possible way, and that's general purpose gateways. Later on, folks with higher levels of fitness and experience will explore other services more quickly, but I've found that the best starting place is over at the left-hand side of the chart on the previous page.

Now let's go to picking a specific service.

The best place for most folks to start is America Online. It's got a system that's easy to use and a broad range of services and connections. Prodigy is pretty good if you're not that concerned with connecting to other services. eWorld is fine if you're on a Macintosh computer. The Microsoft Network is not even open for business as this is being written, so precise comparisons are hard to make.

Here's an easy way to pick the service you should start with. I call it the Magic Factor.

It's a lot easier to go to a new neighborhood if you've already got friends there who can be guide and mentor to you. They can show you around and give you tips about what to do.

The Magic Factor is the friendship factor. To get it to work for you, you need to find out which of your friends and colleagues are already online and where.

Start by going back to your listing of folks who are important in your life. Review the list and see if you want to add any. Then figure out which of them are online.

Go down the list and check off the possibilities. Some you'll know for sure are online. Maybe they urged you to buy this book so you could get connected. With others you'll have to find out.

Now mark those folks who live or work near you, whom you're comfortable with, and who might be online. Decide whom you'd most like to have show you this amazing new world. That person is your Magic Factor. With their help you'll get connected easily, quickly and productively. And you'll pick the service you sign on to first according to what service they use.

There is one thing to beware of, though. Pick someone who's a regular user of one of those easy general gateways. They'll be the person best suited to help you get started. Don't forget the other folks—you can call them (or e-mail them once you're online) for advice and help. But make sure you can start easy.

If your industry has an active bulletin board or online service that isn't on one of the major gateways, find out about connecting to that service as well. You may not want to make it your first choice, but you're sure to want to try it fairly soon.

Now, let's move on to the things you have to do to get connected.

WHAT EQUIPMENT DO YOU NEED TO CONNECT YOUR COMPUTER TO THE ONLINE WORLD?

To get connected, you need a computer, a modem, and a telephone line. You also need the cords and cables necessary to connect all of them together.

Computers

Just about any kind of computer will do to get you connected, but online life will be easier if you have a graphical user interface (GUI) such as the Macintosh, Microsoft Windows, or OS/2. That way you can take full advantage of the features of the online services you'll be exploring.

Modems

By itself, the computer cannot produce the signals that go over a phone line and make sense to another computer. So your computer (and the one on the other end of the connection) needs a piece of equipment called a *modem* (short for modulator/demodulator). A modem translates the signals your computer puts out so that they can move through the phone line and still work. The modem at the other end changes them back again so they make sense to the other computer.

Modems are categorized by how they attach to the computer. There are three kinds:

▶ *Internal modems* are inside the computer. If you have one of these, you'll see a place on the back of the computer that has a telephone jack that your phone line can plug into. An internal modem takes little space and is always with the computer.

▶ *External modems* are outside the computer, and are connected by plugging into the computer's COM (for communications) port. Then the phone line plugs into the modem. The main advantage of an external modem is that it has little lights that tell you things about how it's working; also, an external modem can be used with several computers.

▶ *PCMCIA cards* slip into special slots in the computer. Sometimes these cards function as the computer's memory. Sometimes they're modems.

 Usually, to start, the simplest combination of hardware is the best bet.

Modems are also described by how they handle the data they send and receive. This includes how fast they handle the data, and what standards they meet.

Modem speed is measured in *bits per second* (bps). Bits are small chunks of digital information. The higher the bps rate, the faster the modem will send and receive information. You'll also hear this speed referred to as *baud rate.* That's not exactly correct, but it is common usage. (Baud really means signal changes per minute.) Some common bps rates are listed in the following chart, along with comments.

Modem Speed	Time to Transfer a 500K File	Comments
300 bps	Close to 4 hours	Do not take even as a gift unless you collect antique equipment.
1200 bps	About an hour	Too slow for today's services.
2400 bps	About a half-hour	This is the speed on modems sold with computers recently. Too slow to enjoy most services, but can be adequate for simple e-mail.
9600 bps	About 7 minutes	OK
14,400 bps	About 4.5 minutes	1995's current best buy. Will handle most tasks and services adequately.
28,800 bps	About 2 minutes	Tomorrow's standard. Will be more necessary as services become more graphical.
Higher	Time in seconds	Not too far in the future.

Modem performance, as well, conforms to certain industry standards. These cover many things, such as whether the modem *compresses* information when sending it. Compression is good for two reasons: It decreases the number of bits sent, so you can send more data in the same amount of time. Compression also tends to reduce the number of transmission errors.

What does all this mean to you? You're in one of two situations. Either you already have a modem, or you have to buy one. If you bought your computer after 1992, it's likely that you already have a modem. And that modem is probably a *fax modem*. That means it can send (and perhaps receive) faxes as well as data. In fact, some manufacturers call their modems "Send/Receive Fax Modems." If you got one of these with your computer, then it's probably an internal modem.

If you have a modem with a speed of 2400 bps or more, then you probably have all the modem you need to get started and get an idea of what the online world is like. You may want to upgrade your modem later. Then some of the following advice will apply.

Buying or Upgrading a Modem

You can avoid a lot of hassle later if you begin by planning to buy a modem with both fax and data capability. Fax modems cost only a little more, and you'll be adding flexibility from the start.

You'll see the usual price/performance trade-off. The faster modems with more features tend to cost more. Find out first what transfer speeds are offered in your home town by your chosen service. Most places have 2400 bps service, many urban areas have 9600 bps, and a few can even accommodate the new 14,400 bps service.

Next, decide how sure you are that you're going to use this technology. If you think you're probably in this for the long haul, then buy the best modem you can afford. If you're really uncertain and you just need a modem to get started, buy a low-cost 2400 bps modem or better for right now.

I buy a lot of stuff by mail order, but it's best for you to buy a modem from a local vendor who will install it and make sure that it's working, and whom you can call if you have questions. Modem manuals are notoriously hard to understand. They include paragraphs like this one:

> *It is imperative that you configure your system so that IRQ conflicts are avoided. Upon completing this step, proceed to making sure that your registers are properly set to assure optimal communication. Your modem has 28 registers that are numbered from 0 through 27. We strongly recommend that you review all settings prior to attempting your first connection as this will enhance your ability to diagnose problems and make the requisite adjustments.*

Personally, I find it easier to avoid that sort of gibberish. You can, too, if you buy your gear from a local vendor with a reputation for service and a helpful attitude. I insist that these vendors understand my basic equipment-buying agreement: I will buy from them only if, when something doesn't work right, I can hand it back to them and say, "This doesn't work, fix it." If they can't make it work, I return it.

That's the hardware part. Now let's look at what type of software you'll need.

WHAT SOFTWARE DO YOU NEED?

Answering this question is a bit trickier than for the equipment question. It depends on which service you're going to start with.

Start-Up Kits

If you've selected an easy general purpose gateway (America Online, CompuServe, or Prodigy), your software will come with a starter kit. All you have to do is install it. So if you haven't done so already, order or purchase the starter package for the service you've chosen to start with, before you worry about buying anything else.

Communications Software

If you plan to sign on to a local bulletin board, or use the online service that is running at your business or professional association, or connect with the local library, or any other "dial-up" tasks, then you'll need some general-purpose *communications software*. Most people call it "comm program" for short. There's no need to run right out and buy it now. Get comfortable with the general gateways before you try working with communications software and dialing up to other services.

Here are some good general-purpose communications software packages.

General Communications Software
Windows/DOS Software • Procomm • CrossTalk Mac Software • White Knight • CrossTalk • VersaTerm
This software is available from most outlets. Prices run $50–150.

If you're intending to sign on to any service from your workplace, communications software is probably already set up on your system. Check this out before you buy something else.

When you purchase general-purpose communications software, make sure you're getting something you're comfortable with. The best way to do that is to see what your friends are using on similar machines. Get a friend or coworker to help you run a few sessions with their program. Pick the one that seems easiest for you to work with. Later on, if you find that the software you've picked doesn't do exactly what you want, you can always change programs or add another one.

 Always pick ease-of-use over power when you're starting out.

II

GETTING STARTED

PREPARING FOR YOUR FIRST ONLINE SESSION

At this point you should have the equipment you need. You should have (or at least have ordered) your software. Now it's time to really get started.

The Demo

In this section we're going to get you going on the Information Highway. Just as when you learned to drive, we recommend that you do the first couple of sessions with an experienced user. Then we're going to give you a couple of simple assignments that will help you begin building your comfort level and enjoying the benefits of being online.

This is where you really need your friend, the Magic Factor, that we mentioned earlier. Your next step is to watch your friend run a couple of online sessions. Get an idea of what things will look like when you sign on. This demo session will be on *their* account at the online service. Unless they have a laptop or notebook computer and are willing to come to your office or home, you'll most likely be working wherever they have their computer set up.

When you get together with your friend, explain what you want to do in this session. You may want to show them a copy of this section. Also, before you sign on, choose a *forum* (sometimes called a *discussion group*) that has a topic of interest to you, and a publication (such as a computer-related magazine) or information source (such as a database or online encyclopedia) that interests you. Use the start-up material you've received from the service to see what's available and make your selections.

When you're ready for session one, here's what we want your friend to do—with you right there watching, asking questions and making notes:

1. Sign on

2. Show you the menus and commands they think you'll need

3. Send e-mail to another account

4. Show you how to find a forum or discussion group

5. Show you how to find a publication or information source

6. Demonstrate anything else on the service that they think is neat and interesting

This should not be a long online session. Your objective is to get a sense of how things will likely be when you sign on by yourself for the first time.

Take Notes

During this demo session, take whatever notes you want. Lots of people find that when they take notes on a session, it's best if they write down a description of what they see and then make notes about what they should do or want to do right then. Here's an example: "When I see the flag up on my mailbox in the upper-left corner of the screen, I should move the pointer to that icon and click. Then I can read the mail that's waiting for me."

It's important to describe what you actually see in the demo, because everyone notices different things. Make sure your notes reflect what *you* notice.

Capture the Session

If your friend is willing, ask him or her to *capture* (or *record*) the session so you can review it later.

Capturing a session is done differently by each service. If you're using America Online, for instance, you'll have a Logging Feature that you can use. The objective is to give you a record of the entire session that you can review later. That will help you understand it better and make good notes for next time.

Do It Again

When the demo session is over, discuss it briefly with your friend. Observe another session right then, if there's time.

Now for the next step: actually signing on for the first time.

YOUR FIRST ONLINE SESSION

You've seen your friend run a simple online session. Now it's your turn. This session should be on the computer you will normally use to connect to online services. That means you must have your computer set up and ready, with your modem and software installed. If that's not done yet, do it. Your friend may be able to help you.

Go back and review your notes from the demo session. For this first real session, you have two objectives:

▶ Sign on for the first time and set up your account

▶ Run your first session

It will be easiest for you if this session is as much like the demo session as possible. Add to your notes, if necessary, or make any "cheat sheets" you think you might need.

Cheat Sheets

Most new online users find it helpful in the beginning to have a cheat sheet with basic commands and reminders that they can keep right in front of them. I suggest you prepare one, based on your last session. Most of the folks I've worked with like to have their cheat sheet on a 3" × 5" index card. That way it's easy to have around and revise while they're online. Those old reliable and ubiquitous Post-it notes don't work so well for this, because they lose adhesive after a while and don't stick where you put them. The other problem with Post-its is that they stick to other things (like the inside of your pocket) if you want to carry your notes with you.

Your cheat sheet should include whatever you think is important, but almost everyone includes the commands necessary to exit the service. That way if you get lost or perplexed, the "Get me out of here!" command is right there for you.

Signing On

When you're ready, sign on for your first session. (Some services call this "logging in.") Have your friend right there to answer any questions and provide direction and help.

> **IMPORTANT:** In your first session you'll probably have to enter or choose a password. This is NOT something your friend should know, no matter how friendly you are! You'll read more about passwords in the next section.

Some services, including CompuServe, assign you a temporary password for your first couple of sign-ons, and send you a new password that will be effective when you receive it. Other services simply ask you to pick a password. For right now, pick anything you think will work, or use the temporary password if you have one. In your first solo session in the next section, you'll have a chance to change your password.

In your first real session make sure you do the following:

1. Sign on

2. Set up your account

3. Send e-mail to your friend's account

4. Check out the information source or publication you're interested in

5. Check out the forum you're interested in

6. Practice the commands your friend thinks are important

7. Investigate features your friend suggests are valuable

8. Sign off

Follow-Up

When the session is done:

- Discuss it with your friend

- Make any notes you think you'll need to help you with future sessions

- Add important items to your cheat sheet

Your friend has one more job. That job is to encourage you. The best way we've found for your friend to do that is to send you e-mail. Make sure you let your friend know you need to receive responses to the e-mail you send.

Now you're ready to move on, by yourself, to exploring the service you've selected and getting familiar with the online world.

YOUR SECOND ONLINE SESSION: PASSWORDS AND BILLING

By now you've seen a couple of online sessions. You should be getting familiar with the sign-on process and the basic commands you'll be using for as long as you use the service you've chosen.

Before we go any further and set you to exploring, you need to understand two key functions in a commercial online service: security and billing. That's what this next session will be all about.

Let's start with security.

Passwords and Security

There are people in the world who will take advantage of you and who will do bad things to you. Unfortunately, it's as true in the online world as it is in the physical world. That means you must be conscious of online security, just as in the physical world. Here are some guidelines.

The first three rules of online security are

1. **Never** give your password to anyone.

2. Never give **your password** to anyone.

3. Never give your password to **anyone.**

It's important never to give your password to anyone. Your password is what opens your account. Once someone has that, they can "be" you online. They can run up your bills and do all manner of evil things that you'll be blamed for. This is not good. Fortunately, it's easy to prevent: **Pick a good password, never give it out, and change it frequently.** Interestingly enough, as a practical matter, most folks simply don't do this.

Some systems assign you a temporary password. You should pick your own as soon as you're able.

Some systems ask you to choose a password. Here are some tips for picking a good one:

► It should not relate to anything in your profile (such as your zip code or town or profession).

► It should not be anything that someone can find out by talking to you (your birthday, for instance).

► It should not be your first name or any common first name.

► It should not be the name of a pet.

► It should not be "guest" or "visitor" or "friend" or any similar word.

► It should be alphanumeric, perhaps with a bit of punctuation (for example, epsom!345).

Following these tips will help you meet the first criterion for a good password: It should be something no one else can figure out easily.

You may have to make a decision about whether or not you will make your password part of your automatic sign-on. The advantage to this is you won't have to remember it every time. The drawback is that anyone who has access to your computer can sign on with your name and password.

Another rule to abide by is that your password should be easy for you to remember. Some people remember alphanumeric data easily and well. If you're one of those, fine. Otherwise, you have to factor in your ability to remember.

You may want to piece together a password from family data that's not readily available to others and won't come up in conversation. One friend of ours used to use LAKE15GEORGE. How did she get that? It's the name of a place where her family used to spend vacations, mixed with her father's birth year. All she had to do was remember childhood vacations to remember her password. Another friend used his favorite aunt's birthday and initials, like this: 02M15K32.

What these suggestions have in common is that they're easy for the subscriber to remember—but not easy for someone else to guess, and not easily discovered by one of those files that checks names at random.

> **IMPORTANT:** You will defeat your own security system if you write your password down and keep it near the computer. Don't do that! Pick a password you can remember, and then remember it.

If you forget your password, every online service has a system for getting you a new one. Check the service's documentation, or go online to Customer Service or Member Services and ask them.

Take a minute now and do two things:

► Pick a password for yourself

► Check your documentation for the procedure to change passwords

Billing

Decide on your budget for the amount of money you're willing to spend for online services during your learning time. Then convert it into time by dividing the dollar budget by the basic online rate for your service. Some services have different rates, but this should give you a general idea of how much time you can spend online per day, or week or month.

Then, when you go online, keep watch on your time. In the beginning you'll have to do this consciously, but later on you'll find yourself doing it automatically.

When you're starting out, you may want to check your bill *during* every online session. Most services have a way for you to do that. It's usually tied to the keyword or jump-word BILLING. Most online beginners go through a period of learning during which their bills are fairly high. You can control this by allowing for your learning curve and by watching your bill carefully. As you do that, though, remember to make one of your goals to get online frequently enough to get good at the medium. If your bills are going up, try using shorter sessions, but also try to continue using your service regularly.

Right now, examine the documentation for your service and look up how to check your bill.

The Session

In this session you're going to sign on and do what you did in your last session. You're going to do two other things, as well: select/change your password and check your bill.

Plan for the session by reviewing your notes from your earlier work, making sure your cheat sheet is up to date and that you know how to get to the password and billing sections of your service.

Now you're ready to go online for this session. Here's what you should be doing:

1. Sign on

2. Check your e-mail and send a message to your friend's account

3. Check out the information source or publication you're interested in

4. Check out the forum you're interested in

5. Go to the password section and change your password (if you want to)

6. Go to the billing section and examine your bill

7. Try some other features or areas that strike your fancy

8. Sign off

Follow-Up

When the session is done:

- Review it for what you've learned and what you'd still like to try

- Make notes to help you with future sessions

- Add important items to your cheat sheet

YOUR THIRD ONLINE SESSION: E-MAIL

If there's one single best reason for being online, it's probably e-mail. For most people, nothing else comes close.

Back when computer networks were just starting, the folks who put them in place thought they'd be used for serious scientific discussions. That did happen. But what also happened was that users started exchanging personal as well as professional communications. Soon the emerging "net" was filled with messages from one person to another. That pattern has held true for just about every computer network that's ever been started. E-mail has been the most used feature of the networks, and the feature that most folks mention as the key benefit of going online.

You've already received mail from your Magic Factor friend, so you've got an idea of how this works. In this next session we want to expand your e-mail horizons a bit. But first, let's detour for a quick discussion of why this particular online feature is so powerful.

► *E-mail is personal.* For reasons we don't quite understand, people relate to electronic mail in a very personal way. That works *for* you when it helps deliver your message, but it can work *against* you when folks think you're using the medium inappropriately.

► *E-mail is fast.* It travels at the speed of an electron and usually arrives almost instantaneously.

► *E-mail is easy.* On most systems you can reply by selecting (or clicking on) a Reply feature. In that case all the addressing is handled for you automatically based on the incoming message.

► *E-mail is asynchronous communication,* which means the sender and receiver do not have to be communicating at the same time. Like regular mail, people read it when they want to. You don't have to be present for someone to get your message. That makes e-mail a great way to keep in touch without playing phone tag.

OK, now you known why it's powerful. Let's think about how you can use it.

Earlier, in the section on Basics, you made a list of all your friends who are online. Go back to that list now, and add the e-mail addresses of anyone who's on the same system that you are on. In this online session we want you to send e-mail to each one of them. Just send a simple message like the following:

"Hi. I just signed on to this system and it's really neat so far. Please send me some e-mail so I can get in the habit of staying in touch with you this way."

Before you compose your messages, think about what you're going to say. Think about who you're sending the e-mail to. And plan out what you'll do once you're online to get that job done. Look at the instructions for using your service's e-mail and check the notes you've made about previous online sessions. You sent mail then, and the process will be similar.

Update your notes and your cheat sheet. Now you're ready to go online for your next session.

The Session

Here's what you should be doing:

1. Sign on

2. Check your e-mail and send mail to your friend's account

3. Send e-mail to your other online friends

4. Check out the information source or publication you're interested in

5. Check out the forum you're interested in

6. Try some other features that strike your fancy

7. Go to the billing section and look at your bill

8. Sign off

Follow-Up

When the session is done, do the usual follow-up.

- Review it for what you've learned and what else you'd like to try

- Make any notes to help you with future sessions

- Add important items to your cheat sheet

By now that regular online routine we talked about should be turning into a habit. We'll reinforce that habit in your next online session, where you'll get your first taste of online forums.

YOUR FOURTH ONLINE SESSION: FORUMS

Being online should be feeling more and more comfortable to you about now. You are developing some good online habits and a regular routine. You have exchanged e-mail with several friends. And you have done some exploring of online features—while keeping an eye on your bill.

This will be the last of the guided sessions in which we've set out the purpose and sequence and such. After this you'll be on your own to explore, using the good base of skills you've acquired in these practice sessions. You'll be comfortable with the basic online functions.

In each of the previous sessions you've been asked to check in on a forum. You should have some feel for how things work there, what kinds of topics are talked about and how people tend to respond. In this session you'll make a simple posting to the forum. In the beginning of this book you read that you go online for people, information and business. On most services, forums are the places where all this comes together.

Forums (sometimes called conferences or chat rooms or discussion groups) are where folks who share an interest in a general topic can talk online about it. Most forums are divided into sections in which a larger topic (such as Public Relations and Marketing, for example) is broken down into smaller topics (such as electronic marketing, public relations, creativity and so on).

Forums are managed by folks whose job it is to monitor what the participants are saying, eliminate anything that's inappropriate, and make sure communication flows freely. These managers are called *sysops*, which is a contraction of *system operators*.

For your first foray into the wonderful world of forums, you'll be posting an introduction message—that is, one that introduces you. Most forums have a section for this, but even the ones that don't are always ready for newcomers like you to post a message telling folks who you are and what your interests are. That's what you'll do in this session.

Begin by going back over your notes from the previous sessions when you checked in to a forum that interests you. Go over the documentation supplied by your online service. Find out the exact steps to post a message to a forum on your service. Make notes as necessary, and update your cheat sheet if you need to.

Sample Introduction Messages

Now prepare your message. Something like the following could be posted to a business forum:

> "Hi, I'm Sara Jones and I'm new to this forum. I'm also new to being online. This is all kind of strange and wonderful for me right now. I'm interested in the ways that being online can help me in my career, and I'm really interested in marketing. I'm a sales rep for a trucking company."

Or maybe you picked a forum about a hobby or other special interest. Here's a message that might go on one of those:

> "Hi, I'm John and I'm new to this forum and the whole online world. I'm a private pilot and I joined this forum to find out what I can learn from other pilots and folks interested in aviation. I'm just getting ready to plan a cross-country flying vacation and hope to learn things here that will make it easier."

There are also forums for special groups such as Rotary or meeting planners. If you picked one of those, your introduction message might look something like this:

> "Hi, I'm Joan and I run a small independent planning business out of my home. I'm new to the online world and this forum, and I hope I can make some contacts here that will help me stay in touch with what's going on in the business."

The Session

Your assignment in this next session will be to post an introductory message to the forum of your choice. Your session should go something like this:

1. Sign on

2. Check your e-mail and respond to any messages you've received

3. Check out the information source or publication you're interested in

4. Check out the forum you're interested in and post your introduction message

5. Check out any other features that strike your fancy

6. Go to the billing section and check your bill

7. Sign off

Follow-Up

Don't forget the usual follow-up steps:

- Review the session for what you've learned and what you'd still like to try

- Make any notes you think will help you with future sessions

- Add important items to your cheat sheet

There you have it. At this point, you should be getting a handle on the ways you can use online resources and make them a productive and enjoyable part of your life. Here are the tasks you should be able to do right now:

- Handle sign-on and sign-off easily

- Send and receive e-mail

- Get into a forum that interests you, and participate if you choose

- Check an online information source or publication that interests you

- Keep track of your bill

- Change your password

Even if you stopped right now, you'd be able to get substantial benefits out of your investment of time and money into being online. But you've only scratched the surface. Over the next couple of months you'll be learning about ways that your investment can pay off even more handsomely.

You need to make a commitment now, though, to make the online world a regular part of your life. Make a commitment to yourself to sign on every day for the next month. Try some new things. In the next section of this book are several sections about the various online features to which you've been introduced. We'll help you get better at things you already know how to do, starting with an action plan for things to try and learn.

III

BECOMING
SKILLFUL

YOUR ACTION PLAN

OK, you've spend some time online and have probably found some things that interest you. Your next step is to lay out a plan for the next three weeks. This section will help you make some decisions about where online you'll explore and what kinds of things you'll try. Exactly what you experiment with will depend on which service you're on and what your major purpose is for being online.

A Little Research

Let's start with your online service. Many books have been written about the various online services. Sometimes they're available directly from the service, as they are on America Online and CompuServe. Sometimes you'll find them in a bookstore. So, at this point we're going to suggest that you make a small financial investment. We promise you'll be able to see the benefit that will come to you from it. Find a good, basic book about the service you're using to start out. Buy it. Look through it for ideas and tips that will make your online time more productive.

A Lot of Practice

You also want to figure out just what the real value in the online world is for you just now. In the next three weeks we want you to sign on every day, no matter how briefly. Try something new every day. It doesn't have to be anything complicated.

Look up a magazine article—say in *National Geographic*—about a topic that interests you. Or maybe set up a clipping feature to automatically scan the newswires and save stories that interest you. You might want to plan a trip using the travel service, or try to contact via e-mail or a chat room someone you've always wanted to meet. We'll tell you more about how to use these features in upcoming sections.

Making Your Plan

To start putting your plan together, go back to "The Basics" in Part I and look over those worksheets you filled out there. They'll help you remember what you want to try.

Look at the detailed material on your service. Make a list of things you want to try.

Call up your online friend. Better yet, send him or her some e-mail. Ask for ideas about things to try.

Finally, scan the table of contents and the index for this book. Look for things that seem interesting, exciting or important for you.

Using all your "research," make a list of at least six things you want to investigate or try out online. Rank them in terms of importance.

Your 21-Day Log

We also want you to keep a record of the neat new things you try. And record your progress, too, in learning about this amazing online world. Turn the page, and you'll find a 21-day log for you to maintain as you experiment and explore. Use it to plan longer sessions for days when you'll have a bit more free time or flexibility. Use it to record your notes about your sessions, and new ideas about things to try.

If you're pretty comfortable with online technology at this point, you can probably move pretty fast here. You may even find that you want to jump to the "Moving On" section of the book because something there looks like it'll be really important to you. Only you know if you're ready for that. But even if you are, it's important to get into the daily sign-on habit, so don't neglect that. And even if you're moving fast, make sure you still use that 21-day log.

Why 21 days? Well, our best knowledge and experience about people making significant long-term change in the things they do in life tells us that it takes about three weeks to become comfortable, confident and habituated about a new set of tasks. Stay with it!

Day	Things I Tried	Results, Ideas, Other Things to Try
1		
2		
3		
4		
5		
6		
7		
8		
9		
10		
11		
12		
13		
14		
15		
16		
17		
18		
19		
20		
21		

AUTOMATION

Computers are very good at doing repetitive, routine tasks quickly and effectively. Human beings, on the other hand, are usually not nearly as fast or as consistent. You can put this computer advantage to work making your online life easier, more effective and—last but far from least—less expensive.

You don't want to have to read, write or ponder online any more than you have to. So, your goal is to find which things you do online that should be automated and then get the computer to do as many of them for you as possible.

Tasks to Automate

You should automate the tasks that have these two characteristics:

► Things that are done often

► Things that are done the same way every time

In addition, look for ways to do your reading, writing and pondering *off* line. Those are the things that take time and therefore rack up those connect charges.

Ways to Automate

There are four basic tools for automating online activity: menus, macros, scripts and automation software.

Many services allow you to customize some menus so that you can go directly to the parts of the service you visit often. On America Online, for example, you can customize the Go To menu so that you can go directly to (let's say) the *San Jose Mercury News* with just a couple of clicks rather than a sequence of commands.

A *macro* is a record of several commands assigned to a single keystroke or command. You may be familiar with macros from a word processing program that you use. Many popular applications offer you a way to replace several keystrokes with only one or two. For example, you might set up a macro in your word processing application to enter the signature block at the bottom of a letter. By assigning the key-combination Alt+1 to the steps for that task, the computer will type the entire signature block for you every time you press Alt+1.

Many communications programs offer you a way to do the same thing with communications tasks. Let's say you often check for articles of interest on an online service that you use. The service presents a menu of choices. Once you've reviewed the list and selected the articles you want, you like to delete the list of articles that you've reviewed. To do that, the steps are always the same: M<Enter>M<Enter><Enter>. If you set up a macro for that sequence and assigning it to Alt+1, the computer will execute the steps to delete the list—faster than you can type and without errors.

Let's take another example. Remember that signature block macro we cited earlier? You can do exactly the same thing with your e-mail. Just record a macro to type whatever you normally type at the end of an e-mail communication.

Scripts are a bit more elaborate than macros. In a macro, the computer substitutes a couple of keystrokes for a larger number of keystrokes. When you use a script, the computer waits for the service to do something and then responds with a recorded set of keystrokes.

On major commercial services such as CompuServe and America Online, there are already some scripts built in. For instance, on both services (using their standard graphical software) you can check your mail in either of two ways. You can do it manually, by signing on to the service, going to the mail area, checking for new mail, reading (or downloading) your mail, and signing off. Or, you can select options that let the computer do the work for you. On America Online, for instance, this option is called a Flash Session. Using Flash Sessions can cut substantially your online time spent for routine tasks such as sending and receiving mail. When we tested Flash Sessions recently, we found that it took about a minute using a Flash Session to sign on, send and receive some e-mail, and sign off. To handle the same number of messages manually took about three times as long.

Now you know about macros and scripts, but there are ways to automate even more of your online activity. Entire programs are available to automate your online work. There are two kinds of these automation programs: One kind is an "add-on" to a particular service's standard software. The other kind substitutes an entire communications interface program for the service's standard communications software.

If you're on America Online, you have to use America Online's software. You have no choice. Fortunately, AOL has worked hard at helping you automate your work with Flash Sessions and customized Go To menus. Even so, as you grow more proficient in online work there may be some things that you'd like to automate, but which are beyond the scope of simple menus and such that you're comfortable handling. In that case you should look around for an automation add-on.

> **NOTE:** Often these add-ons are available as shareware or freeware—software made available by its author to the public. You can try it out for free, and you pay a small registration fee if you decide to keep it. Shareware is discussed more thoroughly in a later section, "Forum Libraries."

If you've got something you'd like to automate, chances are that someone else has had the same experience. If that someone else happens to have been a programmer, he or she has very likely written a program to get the job done. All you have to do is find it. You will usually find these programs listed under Utilities or Communications Programs in special forum areas, called libraries, devoted to computing or some similar topic.

So you should search those libraries, right? No, there's a better way. Ask people who've used your service for a while if they use any special programs or utilities to automate tasks. That way you'll not just find out about the programs available, but you'll get valuable, first-hand information about their strengths and weaknesses. Then you can go to the appropriate library and search for or order a file that sounds helpful.

Those techniques—checking the forum libraries and asking others about their experience—will work equally well for America Online and for CompuServe. But with CompuServe you also have the option to get a program that will automate all your forum and e-mail activity.

Remember that, unlike America Online, you can use several different software packages to get to CompuServe. You can use CompuServe's own software (such as WinCIM). You can use a general communications package (such as Procomm or VersaTerm). Or you can use a special package written expressly to automate e-mail and forum activity on CompuServe.

Because CompuServe has been around so long, and because it has so many subscribers, there have been specific automation programs written to make your time on CompuServe more productive. These programs will handle the sign-on function for you, check your e-mail and forum messages, and sign off—all automatically and quickly. They'll even help you check forum libraries more effectively.

If you find that you're doing a lot of e-mail and forum activity, you should consider automating those activities as much as you can.

What to Do to Automate

- Identify the things that you do online that could be automated.

- Customize any menus on your service that will make your online time easier and more effective.

- If your communications software can set up macros or scripts, make one for a routine task. Then use it for a month.

PURCHASING ONLINE

Information isn't the only thing you can buy online. You can buy things, too—from soup to nuts. Online you can check out products you're thinking about ordering and actually order them, as well. If the product is electronic information, that may be delivered online as well. Let's look at the wide world of online shopping.

Malls and Such

Most online services have a special area for buying things—usually called a *mall*. Many things about a mall in cyberspace are like the shopping malls you visit in the physical world. There are lots of stores that offer lots of options. Many of the stores cater to special interests. And you can use your credit card.

There are two ways you can shop for things using the cyberspace malls.

First, you can buy many products outright. Several mall vendors offer computer equipment, for example. You can check the specs for their merchandise and place your order online. Shopping the malls on the major services is most convenient if you use your credit card for ordering, though sometimes you'll prefer to send a check to a physical address. On the major commercial services, your online purchase is a secure transaction with a reputable vendor. And you have the service to go back to if things don't work out.

The other kind of online shopping you can do is for products that you won't actually be buying over the computer—cars, for example. For that kind of product you'll be able to check out specs online and maybe even get a computer demonstration of the product. Then you'll go to a local vendor in physical space to complete the transaction.

Other Vendors

There are other folks selling stuff in cyberspace who aren't in the malls. They sell through e-mail contacts, word of mouth on various forums, and the classified ad features offered on many online services. For example, you may see a classified ad or forum posting that mentions a product or service, and contact them about it. Or you may receive an e-mail from someone with something to sell.

In cases like this it pays to exercise a bit of care before ordering. Some vendors will be names and companies you recognize from traditional stores and advertising. Others will be people who are online a lot and whose names are familiar.

 When you're buying from a vendor that's not in one of the e-mail areas, make sure that you have a way to contact them other than e-mail. A regular postal address and phone contact aren't guarantees against a bad experience, but they'll give you a place to start if you have trouble and the vendor is no longer available online.

Checking Things Out Before You Buy

You can also use online resources to investigate beforehand the things you want to buy. There are two ways to do that.

▶ *Consumer Reports* **and Others.** Just as there are consumer services in the yellow pages, you'll find them online. You can access the well-regarded *Consumer Reports* online, as well as services and organizations such as the Association of Independent Investors.

▶ **Forums.** Don't leave the forums out of your checking and buying process. When you're considering a purchase and want more information about the product or vendor, post a question in the appropriate forum: "I'm thinking about buying _____. Has anyone here done that?" You should get some useful and insightful responses. Remember that the forum libraries, too, may contain files that will help you. Search them for information you need about the products and services you're considering. (You'll read more about libraries in the section on forums).

You may be asking, "What's an appropriate forum?" In this case, it would be a forum dedicated to a particular profession or interest, or to a particular type of product.

Getting Help with Your Travels

Among the many things you can purchase online are travel services. You'll find online travel agents who can help you just as travel agents in an office do. You'll also probably have access to services and systems that will allow you to check out airline fares and schedules yourself, and then make your own airline, hotel, car rental and other reservations directly.

Assistance

There are plenty of online services that offer features for helping you with the management of your investments. In addition to investment newsletters, financial news, and business and financial information, most services provide you with a way to brokerage-type features for buying and selling investment instruments online.

What to Do to Increase Your Online Buying Savvy

- Visit the mall on your online service at least three times. Try to check out different vendors each time.

- Next time you want to make a purchase, try gathering information online that will help you make a better buying decision.

- Experiment with using online travel services and vendors, and look into online investment information and transactions.

CHATTING ONLINE

Most of the commercial services have a *chat mode.* It's called
CB-Simulator (CompuServe) or People Connection (America
Online) or Internet Relay Chat (IRC) or something similar. These
are places online where people talk in real time, in conference
rooms, chat rooms, discussion groups, and the like.

Chatting areas vary quite a bit from service to service, so you'll
have to check exactly what your service has and the rules for
participating. We're including material on chat because it's a part
of the commercial online services that a lot of people really enjoy.

> **WARNING:** Watch out—this is a real time-eater. Online con-
> versations can go on for hours, and do. And, unlike e-mail,
> there's no way to automate the process to keep your bill
> down. At first, be sure to check your bill after every session
> until you have a good handle on how much time and money
> you're spending chatting.

There are two basic kinds of chat-type situations: regular and
conference. We'll cover regular chatting here. Conferences are
covered in detail in the section on Online Conferences that begins
on page 95.

In regular mode you join a bunch of folks in a room devoted to a
particular topic. That topic may be support of cancer survivors,
people living in the San Francisco Bay Area, sports or just about
anything else. There are almost always several rooms going that are
devoted to "adult" topics, as well. Usually you can tell by its
online title what's being discussed in a particular room.

Getting Comfortable in a Chat Room

When you first enter a chat room, you'll see the conversation roll-
ing along. Sometimes you'll be greeted by the room's "greeter." On

some services and in some rooms the greeter is an official role, a person specifically designated by the service. Other times, it will be someone who just likes to greet folks. Watching the conversation for a few minutes will give you an idea of what's going on in the room. You can then either participate or continue watching. You can also leave.

> **IMPORTANT:** If the topic being discussed is something that offends you or makes you uncomfortable, leave the room. All kinds of discussions go on in chat rooms, and sometimes you can't tell ahead of time what you'll find in a particular room. If you don't like the subject, go somewhere else where you're comfortable.

Another situation you may encounter is finding that you've entered a room of "insiders." Those are folks who already know one another and spend most of their time saying hello to people by name and sharing "in" jokes. That happens online just as it does in the physical world. The difference is that online it's much easier to back away and go somewhere else.

You may discover that you want to become a regular in a particular group, signing on frequently and always checking out a particular room to see what's going on and greet friends. Or you may want to just check into different rooms every time you sign on to chat. You can do both—or you may not like chatting at all and choose to stay away.

We've already mentioned that lots of folks think online discussions are one of the really great things to do on the Information Superhighway. It can also be a little scary. One reason is that the conversation in many rooms goes very fast. Lines fly across the screen with several different conversations going on at once.

If you're new, it'll be hard to follow what's going on and harder to keep up. The way to beat that is to refrain from participating until you're comfortable following the discussions. Then ease yourself in.

Private Messages

The other scary thing that can happen in chat is getting messages from someone who makes you uncomfortable. Most systems have some form of *private message* that allows one person to send messages directly to another, and carry on a conversation in private. But unwanted private messages can really upset some folks when they get them for the first time. That won't happen if you're ready. Here's what to expect:

The service will alert you to the message. The alert will be a message (usually accompanied by any bells, beeps or other sounds your computer allows) that says, " _____ is paging you," or something like that. On some services, the message itself will appear, also accompanied by those bells and beeps.

Find your online service's documentation now and review the section on private messages, so you will know how to respond. Look for instructions on

- How to send a private message

- How to respond to a private message

- How to block private messages

Then add the key items to your cheat sheet.

> **IMPORTANT:** If someone sends you private messages that make you angry or uncomfortable, you can ask them to stop. If this doesn't work, take the following steps. First, block their message if your system will allow that. Then send an e-mail or other message to a service representative, guide or other assistant with a description of what happened. Include the name of the sender, what they said, when it happened and in what online section. And be sure to mention if they continued to send these messages after you asked them to stop.

Using a Handle

In many systems you get to use a special name for yourself (a pseudonym) when you're in the chat area. On some systems it's called a *handle;* on others it's called a *screen name.*

The handle you pick for yourself will determine the first impression you make in a chat situation. The way to choose a handle is to decide what kind of first impression you want to make and pick a name accordingly. "Sportsnut" or "Giantfan" would give one kind of impression; "Engineer1" or "Salesguru" would give another. Once you've decided on a handle, use it for a while to see if it has the effect you want. If it does, great. If it doesn't, change it.

Avoiding Sexual Conversation Online

This leads us into a rather sensitive area. In parts of the online scene, folks get together for sexually specific chat or to make connections related to sexual activity. It's also a fact that a large number of online users are adolescents. It is likely, therefore, if you are doing online chatting for any length of time, you are bound to run into some form of sexually explicit conversation. If that's what you want, fine—but if not, here are some things you can do to avoid trouble.

1. Be careful about your handle or screen name. Most female names will draw at least some messages that include a sexual proposition. So if your major purpose online is business, for example, you may want to use a neutral screen name. On services that allow you to have several different names, choose a name that's based on your purpose for going online.

2. Stay away from places where explicit sexual activity takes place. Obviously, wandering into a room with the title "Looking for an Affair" will be like walking into a singles bar. It can be just what you want, or merely interesting, or downright offensive—depending on your personal preferences and style.

3. If you find yourself in a place where things are going on that make you uncomfortable, leave.

4. If you find yourself receiving offensive messages or e-mail, ask the sender to stop. If that doesn't work, report him or her to the appropriate authority on your service.

Getting Started with Chat

We've found most folks do better at getting started in chatting if they use the following procedure.

- First, find a friend who used the chat feature frequently. Talk to him or her about how things work. Be sure to ask if they know of any special rooms that you might want to avoid.

- Once you've done that, go to the chat area you're interested in and just watch. Do this in several sessions. Be sure to know the commands for exit so that you can leave when you want to.

- After you've found a chat room that you're comfortable with, begin participating. You'll usually get a friendly and helpful reception if you let folks know that you're new.

USING MEMBER DIRECTORIES

All of the major commercial services and most other services and bulletin boards have some kind of *member directory*. There are two kinds: those that allow details and those that don't.

America Online, for example, has a directory that allows you to have a personal profile listing your interests, location, type of computer, occupation and other, similar things. CompuServe's directory, on the other hand, will list only your name, account number, city, state and country. (On CompuServe, however, most of the forums have directories where you can tell quite a bit more about yourself if you wish.) You'll have to check your service to determine what directories are available and where they are.

There are two ways that you can use online directories. You can use them to search for specific people and you can use them to tell people about yourself and what you have to offer.

Finding Someone Online

Let's say you want to find a friend who you know is online. You can do this by searching the directory for your friend's name. Normally the best way to do that is by last name and location, if your system gives you that option. Even if there are lots of Smiths, say, in Lincoln, Nebraska, the number of Smiths on your service should be manageable enough that you can come up with a list that is highly likely to include your friend. The trick is to give the directory search as much information about your friend as possible.

Remember that the search function will only look for what you tell it to look for. On most systems, if you look for Ron Jones, the search will not include someone listed as Ronald Jones. Or, if you're looking for someone who lives in Naperville, IL, you won't find that person if they've listed their city as Chicago. That's why last name and state are a good way to start looking.

If you don't find the person you want on the first attempt, try a couple of different combinations of search criteria. If you still can't find them, remember that being listed in a directory is an option on most services, and your friend may choose not to be listed.

You can also search for folks who meet a specific characteristic, such as an occupation or a hobby. Usually, you'll do this in a directory that allows details about its members, but you can do it in basic directories, too, if they include interest categories. Just remember that the system will search for exactly what you tell it to search for.

Listing Yourself Online

Now for the use of service directories: telling other folks about you. Let's consider two services where this process happens quite differently, to see what your range of options are.

On America Online, you have the option to add screen names to your basic account. Lots of folks have separate names for business and personal use. Since you can add a member profile for each screen name, many users have more than one profile.

The general rule on profiles is that they should tell folks the information about you that you want everyone to have, but don't care if anybody has it. Your profile should contain information about you that relates to your purpose for posting it. If that's a business purpose, you should include the business items and keywords that are relevant. You might want to avoid including personal information, however. If it's a profile for personal use, on the other hand, you will probably want to include information about your interests, but maybe about your computer or occupation.

Remember that anyone with an America Online account can get the information that's in your profile. So you don't want to put anything there that will compromise your password, for example, or give the occasional troublemaker a way to contact you (other than online). Here's a way to consider what information is okay to include: If you'd be comfortable with the information appearing in a front-page newspaper story about you, then it's probably safe to include online.

Now for CompuServe. Although its basic member directory limits you to name, account and location information, the CompuServe forums usually allow you to post more detailed information about yourself and what you do. The same guidelines that we just talked about for America Online member profiles apply to CompuServe forum listings as well—but with a couple of differences.

Usually in the members directory for a forum, you'll be able to put lots of information in your listing. Resist the temptation. Keep your listing brief but interesting. When you prepare your listing, lay it out like a newspaper story. Put the most important information first, then the next most important, and so on. That way, if someone only scans the entry, they'll get the stuff you think is most important. Consider posting your information as a series of single lines, instead of a narrative paragraph. That makes it easier for people to grasp the key points.

In most cases, the lines of your listing will all be run together unless you take the following step: Before every single line that you want to stand alone, enter two carriage returns and then add a space.

There's one other thing to keep in mind about the forums' directories. Forums are organized to promote discussion and information exchange about a specific topic or interest. So your listing in the directory for the forum should include information that's relevant to the forum topic.

Getting Aquainted with Directories

Here's what you can do to develop your skill with member directories.

- Make a list of the kinds of member directories that are available on the services you use.

- Search the directories for several friends.

- Search member profiles or a forum directory to find people with a particular characteristic or interest.

- Enter or update a profile or directory listing for yourself.

- Go back to your earlier list of folks you'd like to make connections with. Search the online directories for them.

ELECTRONIC MAIL (E-MAIL)

You've already become accustomed to using e-mail in the Getting Started practice sessions. In this section we'll go beyond that to learn more about this powerful and personal method of communication.

E-mail can have both positive and negative effects on your life and work. For instance, because e-mail can reach folks at their homes or at their desks, that means it gets to you fast. But it also will usually bypass the secretaries, receptionists and voicemail screens that keep traditional communications from getting through when you don't want them to.

E-mail has a strange "status" just now. It has the same importance that long-distance telephone calls used to have. Back then, if someone called long distance, everything stopped until the conversation was handled. That seems to be the case now, somewhat, with e-mail. People seem more willing to respond to e-mail than to other forms of communications. As e-mail becomes more common, that will probably change, but right now the medium is new and exciting and fun, and lets you try some neat things.

How do you use this medium most effectively? Whether you're responding to internal company network e-mail or posting replies to a public bulletin board, there are rules you can follow to communicate more effectively. In your e-mail communications, try your best to be conversational, swift, colorful, and succinct. Let's take a look at these four characteristics.

Be Conversational

E-mail is more like conversation than it is paper mail. You should be informal in e-mail, as you would in conversation. You can even use "almost words" such as *gotta* and *gonna* to keep this conversational flavor in your e-mail messages.

In e-mail you don't have to pay so much attention to all the cues to rank and position that you run up against when you talk face-to-face (called "F2F" in online parlance). That turns out to be good—because it encourages an *exchange* of ideas rather than just *transmission* of ideas. The bad side of that particular coin, though, is that you also *don't* have cues such as facial expression and voice tone to convey shades of meaning. So when you're sending, you have to do that with letters and symbols. When you're receiving, you need to watch for the same kinds of clues.

The letters and symbols used to portray nuance and expression in e-mail are called *emoticons*. They're also called *smileys*, after the little face that looks like this :-). Frowns would be :-(or some variant. (If you have trouble figuring out these smileys, look at them sideways, by tipping your head to the left.) You will find lists of these little darlings in a number of computer books—hopefully, the one you purchased on our earlier recommendation. They're also usually available in digital form on many of the commercial online services. Here are some of the most common:

:-)	=	happy face
:-(	=	unhappy face
8-)	=	happy face with glasses
*	=	kiss
{ }	=	hug as in {{{John}}}
:-0	=	shocked or amazed
;-)	=	winking

Be Swift

To communicate effectively, you must be quick. "Absolutely, positively overnight" used to be the standard for speed. No more. Now folks look for instant response. And folks who are online seem to want response even faster than others.

Fortunately, it's easy to respond quickly to e-mail. There's almost always a Reply option that takes care of all of the addressing for you. Use it. Try to make it a habit to answer your e-mail as soon as you get it. If you don't have the full answer right then, let the other person know that you'll be getting back to them.

Use some of the shortcut abbreviations (acronyms) that lots of folks use. For example, typing **BTW** for "by the way" is quicker and marks you as an online person in the know. Like the emoticons, there are lots of places to find lists of these acronyms. Also, watch for them in your incoming messages, find out what they mean and adopt some of them yourself. Here are some of the more common acronyms:

PMFJI	=	Pardon me for jumping in
BTW	=	By the way
OTOH	=	On the other hand
IMO	=	In my opinion
IMHO	=	In my humble opinion
TIA	=	Thanks in advance
LOL	=	Laughing out loud
ROFL	=	Rolling on the floor laughing
FYI	=	For Your Information
FYA	=	For Your Amusement
<g>	=	Grin
<vbg>	=	Very Big Grin
FWIW	=	For What It's Worth
TTFN	=	Ta Ta for Now

Be Colorful

This one goes hand-in-hand with being conversational. It helps if you've got a distinctive online "voice." There are a couple of ways to develop this.

You can use colorful language that gets your message across quickly and vibrantly. Instead of having folks "going" somewhere, you can have them "slouch" or "stride."

Inject humor into your e-mail. If it's fun to read, people will be more likely to read it—and more likely to remember it. Humor is usually easier if you remember to be conversational. But beware—some humor that works face to face doesn't work in e-mail. A good rule of thumb is that if you normally need a facial expression or tone to convey what you want in conversation, that tone probably *won't* work in e-mail. And sarcasm almost *never* works in this medium.

You don't have underlining, italic, and boldface in most e-mail, so use asterisks to convey emphasis, like this: *Wow!* And use CAPITALS when you need a *lot* of emphasis. Just don't overuse them. Capital letters are LIKE SHOUTING when you're online.

Be Succinct

Try to send short, tight messages. E-mail is a medium of speed, and people get impatient with long posts. A good rule is to keep your posts under 24 lines, which is one screen on most computers. Use short sentences and paragraphs, too. They're easier to understand than long ones.

It's common practice in e-mail to copy the question you're answering or the comment you're replying to, into the text of your response. Don't overuse that. A line or two should be all you need to remind the recipient of what was said. Usually that reminder text is set off in brackets, like this:

> <<How can I find more information on Hawaii vacations?>>
> There are always promotions on these. Ask your travel
> agent. You might want to check here in the online mall
> as well.

Getting Good at E-Mail

Now that you have the basics, here are some suggestions for things you can try to increase your e-mail skills. You've already sent and received mail from friends, so we'll try some different tasks now.

► Try sending an e-mail letter to the editor of a newspaper, magazine, or other publication. Many have e-mail addresses. For those who are online, the address usually appears in the posted articles.

► Try sending an e-mail letter to someone who's not on the same system you are. That message will have to go over the Internet. Your service will have a procedure and an address format for doing this. Find out what it is. Sometimes there is a chapter in books about being online, or about a particular service or the Internet, that tells you how to send e-mail "anywhere." (This capability is a great blessing for folks who have kids in college. The kids may have a free e-mail account there!)

FORUMS

Forums are the clubs of the online world, where people with common interests get together and discuss those interests. Not every service calls these "clubs" forums. They may be called discussion groups or conferences, for example, on your service. But they all have a few things in common.

All forums cover a general topic or address a particular group of people. Here are just a few of the forums on one major service:

- Public Relations and Marketing

- Aviation

- Cancer Survivor Support

- IBM Computers

- Writers

- Educational Research

- Wine

- Cooking

- Journalism

- Law

- Investors

- Religion

- Travel

- Working-from-Home

And each of these forums is divided into sections with more focused interests.

As you can see, the subjects for forums are almost limitless, but forums do break down into four general types. There are forums for personal interests, business and professional interests, special groups, and product support.

Forums devoted to personal interests cover a broad range of interests and needs. Some of them concentrate on hobbies, such as model railroads. Others provide support for folks with specific health and life challenges, including cancer, diabetes, and physical disabilities. Still others cater to people whose special interests are in wine and cooking and other areas that aren't necessarily hobbies.

Business and professional forums are usually named for the industry or profession whose members participate. Some are focused on a function, as for Public Relations and Marketing. Others are for those in a specific profession, such as law, or an industry, such as software publishing.

Some *special groups* have their own private forums or sections of a forum. Access to these is limited and controlled. You'll find special forums for members of a particular association and limited to the members of that association. Others are for members of a particular profession who want to discuss issues that are not appropriate in a public forum.

Technical support forums are a bit different. They generally are organized, run and supported by a company that provides a product or service. The purpose of the forum is to help folks use that product or service more effectively. You'll find online forums for most types of computer equipment and software, for example, where you can ask questions and pick up good ideas about using the product.

Finding the Forum You Want

On most services, you can find forums in three ways.

▶ Most services let you search for forums of interest by using a keyword. This is the way you'll get the most up-to-date list.

▶ The documentation for most services will give you an idea of the available forums—although that list is only current when the documentation was printed.

▶ Other users can direct you to forums that can help you.

How Forums Are Organized

Most forums have two basic parts: *message boards* and *libraries.*

You've already experienced posting messages in your Getting Started sessions. People post messages to the boards, which are a lot like bulletin boards. Other folks respond with comments, disagreements, answers and information.

The messages are organized into *threads.* The threads link messages and responses in the order they were posted as illustrated by the diagram on page 74. This feature lets you more easily follow the thread (or flow) of the conversation.

Messages don't stay on the forum message board forever. Most forums have a limited capacity for messages. (It may be a huge capacity, but it's still a limit.) Every day some older messages are removed from the forum so there is room for new messages. This happens more quickly in some forums than in others.

The power of the information on forums comes from the expertise of the folks you find there. Many nationally known experts participate regularly in online forums, sharing their knowledge and insights. You'll also find many experts who aren't nationally known, at least not yet. (You'll also find a few who only *think* they're experts.)

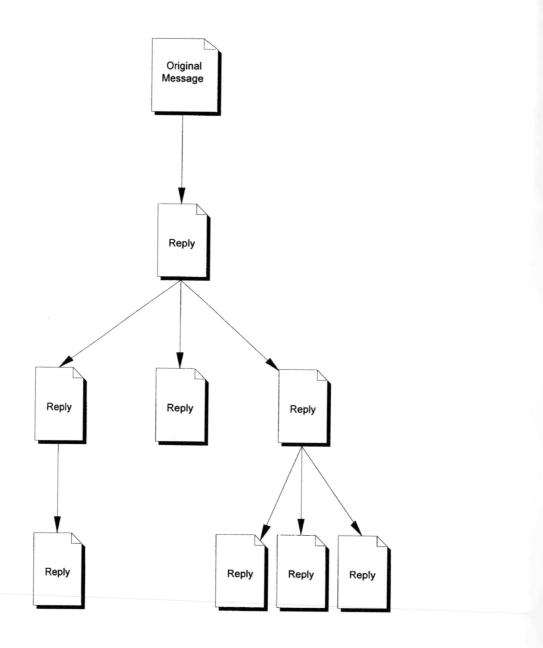

In addition to the message boards, most forums have *libraries*. Those libraries contain a wealth of information and help, in electronic files that have been *uploaded* (see Note below) by members of the forum. Sometimes libraries also contain a complete message thread of particular interest.

NOTE: Let's stop for a minute for a couple of definitions. What do we mean by uploading and downloading? When you send an electronic file via modem from your computer to another computer (and the forum libraries are, in fact, on another computer), you *upload* it. When you transfer a file from another computer to your computer—again, via modem— you *download* it.

The libraries in most forums contain files of all types. These may be programs that will run on your computer, or information files that will be helpful to you. They may contain information about people you can call on for help. You'll find out more about libraries and their contents in an upcoming section.

How you get library files (by downloading) will vary with your service and communications software, so you'll want to examine the appropriate documentation for instructions. Perhaps you watched your friend download a file during the demo session in Part II, in which case you'll have some notes on the process. You should browse the libraries first to see what's available, and then download a file or two that interests you. Most people have a little trouble with this at first. That's OK—if you can hang in there and learn to get these files from forum libraries, you'll have access to tons of valuable information and ideas that are available nowhere else. And be sure to read the upcoming section, "Forum Libraries."

A final word about forums before we move on to some things for you to try. A forum is very much like a community. It has certain norms and rules, some written and some not. We suggest that you just read messages for a while before you post on a new forum. Get a sense of how things are done and who the key players are.

Once you become a forum regular, checking in regularly and sharing information with others, it's likely that you'll develop online relationships with other participants. Those relationships will be among the most exciting and productive resources that you'll find online. You'll discover a group of knowledgeable, friendly, helpful people who are interested in the same things you are. It's one of the biggest benefits of being online.

Getting Good in Forums

Here are some things that you can try in order to develop your expertise in using forums. Try them when you're ready, after you've done the research and investigation we've recommended above.

- Search online for forums of interest to you.

- Try three new forums. Take one at a time. Sign on to it every day for at least a week. If it turns out to be a forum that has value for you, make it part of your regular online sessions.

- Look into a forum library.

- Download a file from a forum library.

IV

ACQUIRING INFORMATION

GETTING INFORMATION FROM PEOPLE

There have probably been lots of times when you had a question that needed an answer, but you just didn't have the reference resources necessary to find it. If you had a friend who knew about the topic, maybe you asked him or her for the answer. Hopefully they'd either have the answer or know where to look.

That can happen online, too. And online you'll have millions of potential friends who can help. Here's what to do to get information from people online.

Dig the Well *Before* You're Thirsty

Don't wait until you have a question or problem to develop online relationships! When you're already a regular participant in a forum or discussion group, folks there will be more willing to dig a little on your behalf. So dig your well of information early, by helping others with *their* problems and questions. If you don't know the precise answer, but you do know where to start searching, tell them that. If it's a sensitive area, or one where the answer is very long or might not be of interest to everyone in the forum, send your message via e-mail.

There may be some people you think might be helpful to you in some way. Find out if and where they are online (or maybe you've already encountered them while chatting or in a forum). Use e-mail. You can say something nice about one of their messages or posting, or about a file they've put in the library. You can compliment them on something they've done that you have used or read about.

Posting Questions in Forums

When you have a question or problem, it's time to marshal the resources of the online world to help you. These are the steps to follow.

1. Clarify your question. Make sure it's clear and to the point, by trying it out on folks you can talk to before you post it. Write the question out, let others read it, and then have them tell you what they think you're asking for. Keep your question as brief as possible and make sure you mention any time constraints that you're working under.

2. Figure out which forums or conferences are likely to have the people who will know the answer to your question. Ask yourself, "Who would have to know this in order to do their job?"

3. Post your question to the forums or conferences you've selected.

4. Check frequently for replies, so you can make clarifications or follow up quickly. Be sure to thank everyone who posts answers. Even if you don't like what you hear, thank them anyway. You don't have to thank them for the material, but you can thank them for taking the time to offer something.

Other Guidelines

▶ It's a good idea to let folks know that you'd like an answer or a *pointer* to an answer. Pointer is online jargon for a reference, or a place to look.

▶ You're more likely to get a response if you include a brief mention of why you need the information.

▶ It's sometimes helpful to give folks other options for responding. But if you give a phone number, remember that people online are all over the world. Make sure that you give a phone that's answered all the time and one that won't disturb you if it rings in the middle of the night.

► Remember that more and more companies are putting their product support online. If your question or problem is about a particular product, see if the vendor or manufacturer has an online forum and ask your question there.

Using E-Mail

If you know of one or two specific people who may have the answer to your question, send them an e-mail request for information. If they're regulars on forums where you post, your e-mail could say, "I just posted a question to _____ that I think you might have an answer to. Please check it out. Thanks."

Some folks don't check forums regularly. If you don't get a response to something posted in a forum, you can try again and send your entire question via e-mail.

When you e-mail a question to a specific person, you're more likely to get a response if you tell them why you think they would have the answer.

Following Up with a Phone Call

Often a phone call is a good way to follow up on a forum-posted or e-mailed question that needs a complex answer. There are times when one-to-one, personal communication is best.

Sometimes you'll be invited to call. If you are, do so, even when you don't think you'll get anything of value. It helps build a relationship and often you'll be surprised with good information. If you're not invited to call, ask permission to. Try setting up a "phone appointment."

What to Do to Practice

1. Go back to the earlier worksheets on people, information and business. Identify the people who might have answers you might need someday, and figure out where they might be online. Use the resources of your online services to do that. Then check out each of the online locations.

2. Try to post at least one helpful response a week on forums that interest you.

3. Send a complimentary e-mail note to at least one person per week for the next three weeks.

FORUM LIBRARIES

In your first few sessions online you got a sense of how forums/discussion groups/conferences work, so you know they're a great way to reach lots of folks with similar interests. In this section, we're going to look more closely at the libraries of files that are available to you in those forums.

Forum libraries contain files related to the topic of the forum. When a forum is divided into sections, the forum libraries are usually divided into similar sections. There are four kinds of files that you can get from forum libraries:

- Information files

- FAQ files

- Shareware

- Freeware

Information

Most of the files in most forums are information files—text files containing information about a specific topic. These files are put into the library by the people who participate in the forum. Some information files are simple listings of information; others are articles or newsletters.

In most cases, you will be able to browse what's in the library of a forum and look for file names, keywords (often including the author's name), the size and type of file and a brief description. All this data will help you recognize what's in the file and whether you can work with it on your computer.

The file name, keywords and description will give you a good idea of the subject or purpose of the information file.

The file type and size will tell you other things. File type tells you if you can actually use the file.

For some files you'll need to own a specific program or type of computer. Make sure you have the equipment and software you need to use a particular file, before you do any downloading. Most information files in forum libraries are text files (sometimes called ASCII files) that will work in most word processing applications. If you download one of these files and have a common word processing program such as Microsoft Word, WordPerfect or the like, you should be able to open the file. Some word processing programs will ask you for the type of file. If your program does this, choose "Text" or "ASCII." Be sure to note the file size, as well. If you're going to download the file into your computer, you need to know about how much time it will take. That will depend on the size of the file in bytes and the bps speed of your modem.

FAQ Files

FAQ stands for Frequently Asked Questions. A FAQ file that's maintained for a forum usually includes basic information about both the topic and the forum itself. If a forum that you frequent has a FAQ file in its library, you will probably benefit from downloading it and looking over the information it contains.

FAQ files are almost always helpful. Get in the habit of reviewing the FAQ file for any forum that you think you may visit often.

Shareware

Some files that you'll find in forum libraries are programs that you can run on your computer. Many of these programs are *shareware*— try-before-you-buy software.

What you'll download will be a fully functional version of the program. You can run it right away. If you like the program, be sure to register it. This usually entails sending a nominal fee (typically less than $100 and often less than $25) to the person who put the program together. Most of the time registration gets you additional benefits such as automatic updates to the program, more complete documentation, and even additional programs. So be fair and send in those registration fees! It encourages the authors of these helpful programs to keep on writing and sharing them.

Don't think that because a program is shareware, it's junk. Some of this software is, of course, below par—as is some commercial software. But a lot of really great tools and utilities are marketed as shareware, including the original version of the popular ProComm communications software, and KwikStat, a really fine statistics program for the PC.

Freeware, Fixes and Demos

In addition to shareware, there are other kinds of free and inexpensive software available in forum libraries.

Freeware is just that, free. You'll find freeware programs in forum libraries that do lots of neat things without costing you anything.

Fixes are usually found in technical support forums that manufacturers use as part of their customer-support strategy. A fix is a program that takes care of a problem occurring in a piece of software or hardware. Usually the problem to be fixed will be described in the explanatory material for the program. FAQ files often refer to common fixes.

Demos are software programs designed to give you an idea of how a particular program works. Unlike shareware, these demos are usually not full-featured; there will be a programmed limit to what you can do with the program or how long you can use it.

Downloading and Uploading Files

To make real use of forum libraries, you have to be able to download and upload files. (Remember, downloading is copying a file from the service's computer to your computer; uploading is copying a file from your computer to the service's computer.)

You can upload and download whether you're using your service's own communications software or general communications software. If you haven't yet seen these techniques at work, this is a good time to grab that friend of yours again and have him or her walk you through a download session. Use the same practice procedure we used in Part II:

- Talk it through and make notes.

- Watch your friend do it and revise your notes.

- Do it yourself with your friend there to help. Then revise your notes and make a cheat sheet.

- Do it yourself.

There's one more thing that you should be aware of before we leave this subject. Many times files are compressed so that they are smaller and therefore take less time to download. This is done, essentially, by taking out unused "space" in the program. The programs that do this are called compression programs.

This matters to you because it may happen that you download a file to run or view, only to find that it doesn't work. That could be because the file has been compressed. In the DOS/Windows world you can spot these pretty easily because most of them have a .zip extension at the end of the filename.

The solution is simple. Decompress the program. But how? To do that you'll need a decompression program, one that puts the file back in its original, larger shape.

If you're downloading files from America Online, there's a real easy way to handle decompression. Go to the Members pulldown menu and set your preferences so that AOL automatically decompresses files that you download. Then the decompression will happen whenever you download a compressed file.

If you don't want to do that, or if you're downloading files from other services, you'll need to use a decompression program. Two good ones are Stuff-It Deluxe (for the Mac) and PKZip (for Windows and DOS). Get a copy of the one you need and decompress those compressed files.

Scan for Viruses

Before we go on, we should talk about *viruses*. The best definition of a computer virus we've ever heard is that it's a program designed to vandalize your system, destroying programs and data. Technically, some of the programs that do this nastiness are called by other names—*worms*, for example. For our purposes, though, the term virus will cover them all.

The major commercial services screen everything for viruses before they put them in forum libraries. That means the likelihood of infecting your computer with a virus from a downloaded file is pretty slim. If you later move on to downloading from other services, though, be sure to find out about their policies regarding the files they post in libraries. Find out how to protect yourself from computer viruses.

What to Do to Practice

1. Start with a forum with which you are already familiar. Make a list of your questions that are related to the subject of the forum. Then browse the forum library looking for files that might be of interest to you. Notice the characteristics (size, type, etc.) of the file.

2. Check to see if the forum has a FAQ file, and look it over.

3. Download at least one file from the library. Download the FAQ file if there is one.

ONLINE NEWS

Online news is different from what you get from radio, TV, or print. Take a look at the following chart for some comparisons.

Area	Online	TV	Radio	Print
Speed	• Fast	• Fast	• Usually fastest	• Slowest
Filtering	• Editors • Wire services	• Editors • Producers • Heaviest filtering	• Editors • Producers	• Editors
Unfiltered Options	• Reports from those on scene or involved • Wire service stories	• C-SPAN	• Live coverage of hearings and such	
Response	• Often immediate e-mail response	• Some e-mail • Call-in lines	• Some e-mail • Call-in lines	• Little e-mail • Letters to the Editor
Customizable?	• Very	• No	• No	• No

You'll get the most from online news sources if you make them a part of the way you typically gather information. Just as you may scan a newspaper every day, you should check your online news sources. In the same way that you tune in to the news on TV or your car radio, you should set a regular pattern of "tuning in" to online news. Following are some of the ways that news is delivered online.

Online Newspapers

More and more newspapers are showing up online. Most offer some version of the same material that is covered by the printed version of the newspaper. Some others concentrate on local or professional events, going light on the "hard" news.

Most online newspapers allow you to send e-mail to their editors and writers. This gives you an opportunity to contact those folks about their articles or about the paper as a whole. Many editors and writers are more likely to respond to an e-mail inquiry or comment than they are to one sent through the paper mail.

News Services

There are thousands of newspapers in the United States, but only a couple of *newswires* that feed them news. In fact, many newspapers take stories from wire services such as the Associated Press and reprint them with very little editing. Many online services offer a way for you to look at these news services yourself. It's a great way to check out what's happening as soon as it hits the wire, and then see how your local paper handles it.

Customizing Your News

Many services offer you an opportunity to customize your news service by having the computer scan the online news sources and select ("clip") articles of particular interest. You specify several keywords that you think will occur in stories that interest you. When you set up the clipping folder, you tell the computer to look for those words and save any stories that contain them.

This is an excellent way to keep up with interesting news about your political interests, or with news about developments and competition in your business or industry. Be careful, though. You'll have to continually fine-tune your selection criteria to make sure you're getting the stories you want. Also, this is an extra-cost feature.

Linkages

Many online services are linking up with traditional news organizations in ways that to benefit both. Here are some recent examples.

► ABC news offered interactive coverage of the 1994 elections on America Online. Two ABC staffers posted returns, projections and commentary online, and folks on "the Net" were able to ask specific questions about races they were interested in.

► Several news and talk shows are setting up connections with online services. If you're online, you can use your service to send in questions and comments while the show is in progress.

► CNN and other broadcasters, including C-SPAN and the Discovery Channel, are posting information online about upcoming shows. This posting may include background information or an e-mail address for online comments.

Special News

There are many specialty news services that are developing an online presence. Investment newsletters and information services were the first to do this, followed closely by sports information services. Chances are, if you've got a special interest, there's a specialty online news service for you on the Information Super-highway—or there will be soon.

What to Do to Practice

1. Check your online service to see what newspapers are available and what they cover.

2. Pick one newspaper and scan it every day for a month. Save any stories that you find interesting, using whatever Save feature is offered by your service and software.

3. Find out if you can set up a clipping folder on your service. If you can, make a simple folder (one or two keywords) and look at it daily for a couple of weeks.

4. Check to see if any broadcast services have a connection with your service. Then check out the connection.

5. If your online service has any specialty information sources that interest you, check them out to see what's there.

ONLINE MEETINGS

Online meetings help people get together, in real time, all at the same time, and all over the world. This is a great way to bring together folks who are in international branch offices or who are traveling

The easiest way to do this is to set up a private room in the chat area of your service, or a private conference room. Then just give everyone who needs to be there the instructions necessary to get to the room. That's really all there is to it.

Several organizations today, including Toastmasters, use this method to bring together people from around the country. They exchange tips, advice and stories. Some business people set up online accounts for their clients, so they can hold online conferences when necessary.

One friend of ours who travels extensively uses this technique to stay in touch with his family. He puts it this way: "Both my wife and I work and travel. Our kids are old enough to take care of themselves, but two are in college out of town, and there are very few times when we're all at home at the same time. So we all have an online account and we get together in a private online room once a week. We catch up with one another and what we're all doing. It works even if we're all in different cities."

Online meetings are a great way for you to "get together" with other people for some real-time communication. If you want, you can even keep a record of the meeting by using the logging or capture feature of your service. Exactly how you do this varies from service to service and also from software package to software package.

What you need to know is that there's almost always a way to record your online activity so you can review it later. Check out the help files for your service and software for information. Ask your friends (including the ones you've made in forums online) for techniques they've used.

What to Do to Practice

1. Find out how to set up a private chat room or private conference room on your service.

2. Organize a small meeting with a couple of friends or business colleagues.

3. Hold the meeting.

ONLINE CONFERENCES

People, and people sharing information, are big benefits of being online. Most of the time your contact with others will be through forum postings and e-mail. But there are some more formal occasions when people actually "get together" online. This is the *online conference.*

Online conferences are different from online meetings in that the conference has a "speaker" or presenter with whom you can interact in real time. That speaker can be a celebrity—Tom Clancy, for instance, has participated in online conferences about his books. Or the speaker can be someone who is knowledgeable about a specific topic, but hasn't achieved celebrity status. Sometimes the speaker is a whole panel of experts. For example, your author has been the speaker at several online conferences about the topic of doing business online.

Online conferences can bring together experts and participants from all over; geography is not a limiting factor. In addition, scheduling is less of a problem. That's because the speaker doesn't have to travel to the conference, or even be in a particular place. He or she only needs to be able to sign on to the service.

The Players

Here's how this usually works: There are two (sometimes three) official roles to be played. One, of course, is the speaker. He or she will often make a brief presentation and then answer questions. Sometimes there is no presentation and the entire session is devoted to questions.

There is usually a host or moderator, as well. This person has the job of making sure that the conference moves along smoothly. Often there are rules for participants to follow, and the host enforces those. Participants are asked to do two things: post a single "?" when they have a question, so the host will know to call on them; and put the letters "GA" at the end of any postings to signal everyone that they're done.

Sometimes the host splits the moderating duties with a "gate-keeper" or "sergeant-at-arms." When that happens, the second person is usually responsible for greeting all new participants with a private message that tells them the rules of the session. In addition, the gatekeeper is responsible for enforcing the rules, leaving the host free to concentrate on how the meeting is going. Here's a sample private message greeting a new participant to an online conference:

> "Hi. This is a moderated session and here are the rules. If you have a question, do not type it directly. Instead send it via Instant Message (IM) to me. If you don't know how to do that, respond to this message with a ? I will group (and sometimes rephrase) questions to ask our guest. If I don't get your question right, send me an IM and let me know. Thanks for participating and following the rules."

Public or Private

Conferences can be either public or private. Public conferences typically happen in designated conference areas on a service, and to use these areas you need formal permission from the folks who control it (the service, the sysop of a forum, etc). Most active forums have regular conference activity. They usually post information notices about upcoming conferences. Also, some services, including America Online, post notices of interesting conferences as part of the opening or welcome menu.

Private conferences are like public conferences, except that participation is limited. They can be held in official conference rooms or in private chat rooms. Usually private conferences are publicized via e-mail or some other nonpublic mode.

If you decide to set up a private conference, you will have to take care of all the details that otherwise would be handled by more official folks. We recommend that you use the speaker/moderator/gatekeeper format if you can; it's a lot easier for all concerned.

Free Conversation

Online conference-goers will usually want some time to have general conversation without the control of the moderator. We suggest that your online conferences allow free conversation before a conference session begins and for the last third of the scheduled conference session. For example, if you schedule a one-hour conference, you might plan to allow 20 minutes for free discussion at the end of the conference. That way folks can take the conversation in whatever direction they want, but the speaker will still be available to participate and answer questions.

What to Do to Practice

1. Find a conference that interests you on the service you use. Look for announcements of conferences in a forum you frequent.

2. Attend a conference and watch how things work.

3. Attend a conference and participate in the discussion.

ONLINE PUBLICATIONS

It used to be that you could get your favorite magazine in two ways. You could subscribe and receive it by mail, or you could make a run to the newsstand every month and pick up a copy. Now there's a third way. Every day more and more periodicals start online editions. Newspapers, magazines, newsletters and tip sheets are all showing up in commercial online services. That means benefits for you.

Online publications are as close as your computer. You can scan them online or even read them thoroughly there, from beginning to end. You can download stories that interest you and, in some cases, search back through the archives for related stories or more interesting tidbits. In some cases, you even have access to background information that's not available to readers of the printed edition.

Newspapers and Magazines

Increasingly, newspapers and magazines have online editions. Check your service to see which ones are available to you. Publications are available free, or free after signing up, or by subscription. Free means available to anyone. A more detailed edition, one with special information or benefits, is available only to subscribers.

Here are a few of the newspapers and magazines currently online.
If you don't see your favorite here, don't despair.
More are showing up online every day.

Advertising Age	New Republic
American Woodworker	New York Times
Atlanta Journal & Constitution	Newsday
Atlantic Monthly	Newsweek
Backpacker	Omni
Business Week	Orlando Sentinel
Car and Driver	PC Computing
Chicago Tribune	People Magazine
Christian Reader	Playbill
Connect	RI Horizons
Consumer Reports	Road and Track
Crain's Small Business	San Jose Mercury News
Cycle World	Scientific American
Elle	Stereo Review
Entertainment Weekly	Time
Flying	U. S. News and World Report
Home Office Computing	U.S. News & World Report
Investor's Business Daily	Washington Post
Kiplinger's Magazine	Womans Day

Specialty Publications

In addition to the general newspapers and magazines, there are a lot of specialty publications available online. If you've got a special interest, look for a specialty newsletter or other publication that you can get online. Some publications, in fact, are now becoming available in electronic form only. For example, your author publishes a newsletter called *Cyberpower Alert!*, about doing business online, which has no printed version at all. Some online publications cost less in their electronic form than in their printed form.

Archives and Extras

One of the major advantages of an online publication is having access to its archives. Anybody who's ever hunted through a stack of old magazines looking for an article they just *knew* was there somewhere can see the benefits of this. Archives let you search past issues for specific keywords. You can then retrieve and read or download articles that include (or are indexed by) your keyword.

Some publications also list background or supplemental information that's available, related to a particular article. For example, an article about a new product might include information about how to retrieve the news release the manufacturer sent out. Or a story about a political speech might also tell you how to retrieve the full text of the speech.

What to Do to Practice

1. Make a list of newspapers and magazines that you currently read at least once a year, and check your service to see how many of them are available to you online.

2. Pick three publications to scan at least once a week for three weeks.

3. Choose an online publication that has an archive file or is searchable in some way. Search for articles of interest to you.

V

MOVING ON

YOUR ACTION PLAN

By now you should be proficient in the basics of the online world with your first service. You have made the Information Superhighway a regular part of your life. But you've only just put your toe in the waters of possibilities.

In the last part of this book we'll cover some things that you can do to move on into even more rewarding and productive use of the online world. You may have already tried some of them and made notes in your log.

The sections in Part IV are different from the ones you've read so far. Instead of specific suggestions about what to do, we'll just give you brief descriptions of some other features of the online world that you may want to check out. As you think about what to try, refer back to the chart we included in the "What Kind of Services Are Available?" section. It listed various services and their relative degree of difficulty for most people.

New software and services are being introduced all the time that make online communication easier, so the more advanced features are rapidly getting easier to work with. Even so, take care not to move too fast as you explore and learn—unless there's a really compelling reason to do so. Like almost everything else in life, developing the skills necessary to get the most from the online world is best done in small steps. That way you're more likely to succeed, as well as keep on learning so you ultimately get the most you possibly can from this exciting technology.

For now, let's proceed in somewhat the same way we did when you began the 21-day Getting Good program. To put together your Moving On plan, take these steps:

► Go back to "The Basics" section in Part I and find those people/information/business worksheets you filled out. Scan them for ideas about what you still haven't tried to find or do online.

► Look at the detailed material on your service. Make a list of things you want to try.

► Call up your online friend. Better yet, send your friend some e-mail and ask for ideas about more advanced things to try.

► Check your log from the last 21 days. Did you make notes about things you wanted to explore?

► Ask some of the folks who are online about interesting things they've done or services they've tried.

► Scan the table of contents and the index for this book. Look for things that seem interesting, exciting, or important for you.

Once you've done the above, on the next page make a list of at least six things you want to try or check out online. Rank them in terms of importance to you. The remaining sections in this book will help you add to your list, and give you guidance in moving on to these more advanced areas.

1. _____

2. _____

3. _____

4. _____

5. _____

6. _____

Notes:

OTHER GENERAL PURPOSE GATEWAY SERVICES

If you're comfortable with the first basic online service that you chose, then you may have already looked into (or may want to try) other services. You'll find that the various online services have their own strengths and weaknesses. Each one does some things well and other things not so well. Their costs vary, too. By this time, however, you're something of an online veteran. You'll find that it's a lot easier to learn about a second or third service than it was to get acquainted with the first one.

Using the charts and other material you've gathered to use in this part of the book, see what other services you want to try. Most of the commercial services have a free trial period. Some will even send you communications and other software or let you sign up via modem.

As you try new services, think back to the process we used for getting you started on your first service:

- Start with small steps.

- Get help from your friends.

- Build each session on what you learned from the session before.

Be sure to go back and review what we said in your second online session, about how to keep your billing under control.

And keep that spirit of adventure and exploration as you move on. New things are cropping up online all the time, so there are always new things to do and to try. Have fun!

BULLETIN BOARDS

Bulletin boards (BBSs) come in all sizes and specialties. There are thousands of them around the country. A recent, reliable industry estimate is that there are more than 30,000 bulletin boards.

When to Use a BBS

Bulletin boards always have their own unique character. Some are strong general-purpose information sources that offer a wide range of services to subscribers; the Cyberia board is a good example. Others, like The WELL in the San Francisco Bay Area, thrive on hip and intellectual "conversation." And some are just hobbies run by an individual out of their basement. Some bulletin boards are free; others charge fees. Many organizations have bulletin boards, as well. Several associations have set up simple BBSs to allow members to exchange e-mail and information. City and county governments and other civic organizations have bulletin boards that help you find out about the services they offer.

Remember that bulletin boards are truly individual operations and reflect the priorities, interests and prejudices of the founder. Take Cyberia, for example. It offers a broad range of services, but its main focus is business. The board also has a strong "zine" section where you can pick up the digital equivalent of small-press magazines. In general, bulletin boards either have a geographical emphasis, or they focus on a "purpose." You'll get the best use out of them if you use this fact as a starting point for your exploration.

How to Find Them

If you're approaching your search from the point of view of an interest or professional need, ask your online friends what bulletin boards they like. Often the people you converse with in forums and the like will have some of the same interests as you, and bulletin boards they've found interesting will be interesting to you, too.

If you're taking the geographical approach, you should of course check with your online acquaintances—but you've got some other information sources to use, as well.

▶ To find bulletin boards in your home town, check out the local computer publications. Most areas have these, usually free and available on newsracks around the area. Bulletin boards often advertise in these publications and tell you something about what they have to offer.

▶ When you're traveling, you can find lists of bulletin boards around the country in two magazines, *Online Access* and *Boardwatch*. One or both of these should be available at a large newsstand or a bookstore that has a large selection of computer books.

Be Cautious with Downloaded Files

As a general rule, don't expect bulletin boards to do the same degree of personal or software screening that the general purpose gateways do. Most BBS operators don't have the time, and many are running the board simply as a hobby.

So be very wary of downloading software from a bulletin board—be more cautious than you would be with software downloaded from a major forum library. Almost anything you might find on a board is usually also available either from the larger commercial services or from shareware catalogs. In either of those places, the screening is likely to be better.

We are *not* knocking BBS operators. Most of them are good and conscientious folks. Many of them do carefully screen the software that's available for downloading. But it only takes one nasty virus to cause you no end of grief. And there's no easy way to sort out in advance the good, careful, safe spots from the dangerous ones.

SPECIAL PURPOSE GATEWAYS

If you've got a need for a lot of special information about a particular topic, then you'll probably want to try any of the many special purpose gateway services that offer specific information. There's almost always a traditional source available for the information you want, and as time goes on, more and more of those sources are becoming available online. This information is maintained in databases, libraries, encyclopedias, catalogs and the like.

There are a few principles to follow when you look for databases and other information sources online.

► If there's a printed information source, there's probably an online database. If you can't find one now, check again in a couple of months.

► Many trade and professional associations have online services. These services often include library or database information that you won't find elsewhere. Look to see what's available for your association.

► Before you sign up for a special purpose gateway, check your own general purpose gateway. Many special information sources are available online through the general services. DIALOG Information Services, for example, is available from Delphi, and in part through Knowledge Index on CompuServe. Checking out a special service first through a general service will give you an idea of what's available—without having to pay set-up fees that are often quite hefty.

Special purpose gateways often offer their own software to help you access their information efficiently. Try the system with your own software first. If things are really difficult for you, then go to the special software. The trade-offs here are that you'll have to learn some more software and you'll add more data to your computer's hard drive.

 With any service you want to use, always use the billing control practices we've already talked about. And, to keep costs down, automate everything you can.

The next section gives you a little more help with accessing databases.

TAPPING INTO DATABASES

As you explore the online world, especially when you're looking for information, you'll encounter a number of databases. Here's what you need to know to make the best use of these powerful resources.

What's a Database?

A database is an ordered collection of information that you can search. An online database is similar to a database that you might create on your own computer. For example, you may work with a business database on your company's network, that includes the names of your customers and their ordering history. Or you might have a database of recipes on your home computer. Online databases are a lot like that, and they come in two forms.

Some databases are part of the online service itself. For instance, the member directory maintained on most services is a database. The information is stored in an ordered form, and you can search it using various search criteria. Other standard databases on online services include access numbers, commonly asked technical questions (FAQ), and other information.

Many databases are provided by information vendors. Here's the way that works: An organization or individual compiles a collection of usable information; for example, the Data Courier company has collected information about articles that appear in over 800 business journals. The database includes the name of the author, the title of the article, descriptive material, an abstract, and sometimes the actual full text of the article. The company then makes the database available in searchable form through various channels.

The Data Courier database of business journal articles is called ABI/INFORM. It's available through a number of channels including the DIALOG Information Service. Here's a description of that database:

The ABI/Inform Database provides international coverage of 800 journals on banking, insurance, real estate, accounting and finance, marketing, data processing and telecommunications. ABI/INFORM is a popular database for management and administrative topics. The database includes informative abstracts that summarize the contents of the original journal article.

If you have a subscription to DIALOG or are a member of Delphi, you can dial in to DIALOG's computer and search the ABI/INFORM database to find out what articles have been published on a particular topic.

Database Examples

A-V ONLINE: Information on all nonprint media (films, transparencies, videos, slides, etc.) covering all levels of education.

ABI/INFORM®: Business practices, corporate strategies, and trends.

ACADEMIC INDEX: General interest, social sciences, and humanities literature with an emphasis on academic journals.

AGELINE: Indexes journals covering social gerontology.

AGRICOLA: Worldwide information on agriculture. 1970 to present.

AMERICA: HISTORY AND LIFE: Wide range of information on U.S. and Canadian history.

ART BIBLIOGRAPHIES MODERN: Comprehensive coverage of modern art.

ART LITERATURE INTERNATIONAL (RILA): Worldwide historic coverage of Western art.

BOOKS IN PRINT: Currently published, forthcoming, and recently out-of-print books.

BRITISH COMPANY DIRECTORY: Listing of every limited liability company in England, Scotland, and Wales.

BUSINESSWIRE: Unedited text of news released from over 10,000 U.S. organizations and corporations.

CAB ABSTRACTS: Detailed summaries of worldwide agricultural and biological research.

CHEMICAL BUSINESS NEWSBASE: International trade and business coverage of the chemical industry.

CURRENT BIOTECHNOLOGY ABSTRACTS: Covers all aspects of biotechnology.

DISSERTATION ABSTRACTS ONLINE: Abstracts of all U.S. dissertations since 1861 and citations for some Canadian dissertations.

ERIC: Research reports, articles, and projects significant to education.

GPO PUBLICATIONS REFERENCE FILE: Publications for sale by U.S. Superintendent of Documents.

HARVARD BUSINESS REVIEW: Complete text of the Harvard Business Review.

HISTORICAL ABSTRACTS: Article summaries of the history of the world from 1450 to present.

LEGAL RESOURCE INDEX: Indexing of over 750 law journals and reviews.

LIFE SCIENCES COLLECTION: Coverage of research in biology, medicine, biochemistry, ecology, and microbiology.

LINGUISTICS & LANGUAGE BEHAVIOR ABSTRACTS: Abstracts of the world's literature on linguistics and language behavior.

MAGAZINE INDEX™: Index to articles in over 400 general-interest U.S. magazines.

MARQUIS WHO'S WHO: Detailed biographies on nearly 75,000 professionals.

PAIS INTERNATIONAL: Broad-based source for all areas of public and current policy.

PETERSON'S COLLEGE DATABASE: Provides descriptions of over 4,700 colleges and universities.

POLLUTION ABSTRACTS: Information on pollution, its sources, and its control.

PR NEWSWIRE: Complete text of news releases covering entire spectrum of news.

PsycINFO®: Leading source of published research in psychology and behavioral sciences.

PUBLIC OPINION ONLINE (POLL): Comprehensive collection of public opinion surveys conducted in the United States.

QUOTATIONS DATABASE: Omnibus file of literary, political, and other quotations of note.

SOCIOLOGICAL ABSTRACTS: Worldwide coverage of sociological research.

STANDARD & POOR'S CORPORATE DESCRIPTIONS: Information and news on over 12,000 publicly held U.S. companies.

STANDARD & POOR'S NEWS: Financial news on U.S. public companies.

STANDARD & POOR'S REGISTER—BIOGRAPHICAL: Information on approximately 72,000 key business executives.

TRADE AND INDUSTRY INDEX™: Indexes of popular general business publications and industry trade journals.

In addition to these formal databases, there are also collections of information out there that meet our definition of a database but don't go by that name. One example is the information available to readers of the online edition of the *San Jose Mercury News* on America Online. You can search articles by keyword, or call up additional information on articles that you find.

Databases can give you lots of good information. And information is a powerful tool. All you have to know is where to find it and how to use it.

Where to Find Them

Databases are available in plenty of different places. The ABI/IN-FORM database, for instance, is available through DIALOG as well as a number of other online sources.

This flexibility can get a little tricky. That's because sometimes one service makes information available through another service. DIALOG, for example, makes a limited number of its hundreds of databases available through the Knowledge Index on CompuServe.

So for ABI/INFORM, you can access it with your subscription to DIALOG, or use one of the other services that have it available, or use Knowledge Index on CompuServe. To make things even more interesting, this same database is available at many traditional public libraries on CD/ROM. Is the information the same in all these places? Yes and no. The core information of course remains the same, but your options for searching will differ, and the fields you can display may vary from place to place.

To make things less complicated, find databases of interest to you by asking your friends, online and otherwise, what databases they use. Then check out the directory of features on your online service to see what kinds of databases are available.

A good book to give you an idea of what's out there is *The Information Broker's Handbook* by Sue Rugge and Allen Glossbrenner. This book is aimed at folks who want to start a business doing research for profit, but it includes a ton of good information useful to anyone about what's available in databases and how to search for it.

Useful Tips

Database searching is somewhat of an art form. Be prepared to spend some time learning what you're doing and then practicing. Get a friend to help. Or find a good information broker and buy a couple of hours of their time to teach you.

Remember that most databases are searchable by keyword, which means you need to have an idea about how the information in the database is classified. The easiest way to figure this out is to look up the citation for an article that's exactly what you want. Study how it's classified, and search for other articles with the same classifications.

SCANNING AND SEARCHING: KEEPING UP IN YOUR FIELD

We're sure you don't need to be told about how hard it's getting to keep up with all the information related to a particular profession or industry. It seems that every day there are more magazines, books, videos, newspaper stories and more that demand your attention. Lucky for all of us, online services can help us stay current.

You can use online resources to help you stay on top of important events, people and information. Use information sources that fit your lifestyle and that are easy to use. You'll want to develop a mix of *scanning* and *searching* techniques to get the most from your information-gathering time.

Scanning helps you get a broad view of topics that interest you. It will help you spot trends and connections. Your daily newspaper and weekly news magazine are great scanning tools. They'll alert you to things that may be of interest, in addition to what you may have readily identified as applicable inside their pages. Likewise, you can scan publications online to see what interests you. Just go to where they are online and look around. Forums, too, can help you scan. By examining the headers on forum messages, you'll get a broad picture of what concerns your forum participants.

Searching is a little different. When you're searching, you know in advance what kinds of information you're looking for. The trick is to spread your net wide and haul in as much as you can. With their search capabilities, online resources are great at this.

As described in the "Online News" section, consider setting up a clipping folder to automatically gather news of interest to you right off the newswires. Several news-scanning services are available to you; these often will deliver news stories that match your specified profile to your e-mail box on a daily basis.

Clipping Services

These will scan newswires and publications for you and select stories based on a profile you select.

HeadsUp

A service of Individual, Inc. Delivers custom news to your e-mail box or fax machine every business day. (800)-414-1000

Executive News Service

On CompuServe. Clips stories with keywords you select from selected newswires.

Newshound

On America Online. Clips news stories based on your criteria.

Many online services also have data files that you can search for items of professional interest. You might do a regular monthly search for articles published recently in your field of expertise. This is a great use of the computer, which is a far better and faster searcher than you are. All you have to do is learn how to do a basic search for articles in your field, and then do that same search every month.

Remember that the information you gather from online sources is in digital form. That means you can search it with your word processing program and with other tools, looking for a specific word or phrase. You can also quote from material you've gathered online, by cutting and pasting from it using your word processing application.

Your Plan for Scanning and Searching

It's easiest to keep up if you have a specific plan for doing so. Here's the outline of a plan that works for a lot of folks.

Daily:

- Scan your local newspaper and a national daily publication, looking for articles of interest. (National dailies include the *Wall Street Journal, New York Times, Washington Post,* and *USA Today.*) Clip articles that interest you and drop them in your interest folder. Interest folders can be of general interest or specific topics.

- Check your online services for items of interest. If you're using a clipping or headline service, scan the results you get from it. Clip items that spark your interest and put them in a file on your computer.

- Read as many articles as you have time for today.

Weekly:

- Scan a general news magazine and a general business weekly for articles of interest. Read the articles you have time for.

- As time permits, read articles you've clipped during your daily scanning.

Monthly:

- Scan trade and specialty business magazines that are important to you. Clip articles of interest and read them as time permits.

A great way to stay on top of issues in your industry is to collect copies of the tables of contents from key trade publications. Then scan these tables of contents whenever you need the location of a specific article.

- Review your clipping folders for items of interest that you know you want to keep. Set up a simple filing system so you can find articles when you need them, with no hassle. Look at your folders for last month, as well.

- Be sure to set aside at least an hour for this review.

Most filing systems that people develop for "keeping current" are too elaborate—they're so complex that they don't get used. Consider a simple method that organizes things by topic and date. It's usually easier for most folks to sort through a folder when they need information than it is to find time to type up cards for a sophisticated computer indexing system. Opt for ease over power, to ensure that you use this tool.

The art of "keeping up" consists of having a *regular* reading and scanning habit. Your routine must include daily review of material, coupled with some kind of simple clipping and filing system, plus a regular, more extensive review. Remember that your brain is a connection-making engine. Trust it to *remind* you of things you've read. Similarly, your computer is a powerful and tireless searching tool. Use it to *find* information for you.

Keeping up is one of the necessary professional survival skills. Online services can help you master the art of keeping up, so you have more time to use the information you find.

THE INTERNET

In the last couple of years, a world that used to be known only to researchers and computer aficionados has made it to the cover of *Time* magazine. That world is the Internet.

In this section, we'll look at what the Internet is, what it can do for you and why we've waited until now to talk about it.

What Is the Internet?

The Internet is a network of networks. To understand its range, you have to understand a bit about how it developed.

Back in the 1960s, the cold war was in full cry and U.S. military analysts were concerned about what would happen to government communications in the event of a nuclear attack. They were especially worried about how a centralized communications system could be easily rendered useless with a single nuclear bomb that hit a single location. So the analysts went to the scientists and asked them to design a system that could survive one or several nuclear hits. It had to be decentralized. And it had to be able to function without centralized direction of any kind.

The scientists took a then-new technology called *packet switching* and began by linking up four academic research locations. And the idea worked. That was the origin of the Internet, less than 30 years ago. But it was *only* the beginning.

Pretty soon it became obvious to the people running the new network that you could use it for a number of things. They could use it, for example, to let researchers share their findings. That sharing could happen almost instantaneously, regardless of the researchers' location. They could also use the network to allow a researcher at one location to employ a powerful computer at another location, and thereby make more efficient use of scarce computing resources.

That was the official, organizational development path. But there was another development path happening, as well, and it was keyed to electronic mail. It didn't take folks long to figure out that if you had a network that allowed you to share research findings with someone on the other side of the country, you could also share other information—everything from birthday greetings to opinions about a colleague to political arguments.

The network's users started communicating with one another and that changed things considerably: e-mail became the most used feature of the Internet. And the relationships that developed among people on the net via e-mail helped establish the character of the Net.

The Net grew. From four U.S. sites in the late 1960s it mushroomed to 80,000 *hosts* (another word for computers) and about 600,000 users worldwide by 1989. That's impressive growth—but the real explosion was to yet come. Beginning around 1989, two things started to happen. First was the development of a number of helpful tools that facilitated use of the Internet. And second was a dramatic increase in commercial presence on the Internet.

In 1991, three independent commercial organizations—Alternet, PSINet, and CERFnet—formed the Commercial Internet Exchange (CIX) and began transferring traffic among their customers without use of any government-funded intermediary. Up until then, commercial traffic had not been possible because it was banned from government-funded parts of the Net, so CIX's activity was an important development.

From 1991 on, commercial presence on the Net increased, and there was a move to free the Internet from dependence on government funding. Today commercial connections are the fastest growing part of the Internet. One of the reasons for that growth is that the Internet is becoming easier and easier to use. And a primary reason for that improvement is a product called Mosaic.

Let's begin our look at Mosaic by first introducing you to the World Wide Web, which allows you to "window shop" around the Internet's resources. In 1992, the World Wide Web (also known as WWW, the Web and W3) was invented by Tim Berners-Lee and a team at the CERN laboratory in Switzerland. The WWW incorporates a technology called *hypertext*. Hypertext links parts of a document with other parts of a document, or with computer commands or any number of other things. Most computer help files use a form of hypertext. In those files you'll often see certain words that are highlighted in some way, often with a different color. If you click on those words with your pointing device you get to see a definition of the word, or you may be sent to another part of the help file. Those links are hypertext, and the programs that let you jump around among hypertext files are called *browsers*.

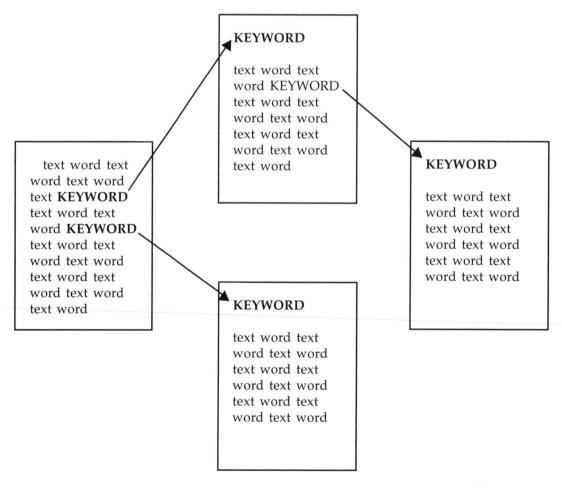

The first browsers for the WWW were text-based browsers; one of the most popular was called Lynx. But the exciting Mosaic browser is a multimedia browser. With Mosaic you can see pictures and click on key icons, just as you can in a Mac or Windows computer, and move around using the hypertext links connected to those elements. Mosaic even uses sound and movies in a multimedia environment. In fact, you can think of Mosaic (and other new graphical browsers such as Netscape) as a sort of Windows-like connection to the Internet.

The development of browsers like Mosaic have made using the Net easy. Until the development of the Web and graphical ways of moving around it, the Net was mostly the domain of people who were willing to learn various sets of complex commands. With the newer, more intuitive tools, the Net has become easy to use by just about anyone.

By April 1994, it seemed just about everyone was showing up on the Net. By then the Net had about 2.5 million hosts and 20 million or so users. The area of greatest Internet growth remains commercial activity. Using the Web, companies are setting up electronic storefronts on the Internet, where you can browse (sometimes seeing actual pictures of merchandise) and even order things.

Other organizations, as well, are on the Web. The White House is there, and NASA, and a host of other government and public service organizations. It's a powerful, fast-growing and exciting environment.

If It's So Powerful, Why Wait to Get On It?

Before you decide to rush right out and get on the Internet, you need to know that it's still not quite as easy as firing up the old computer and tapping a few keys. Although intuitive graphical software is now available, it's still not easy to set up a connection to the Net. And the Net remains somewhat like a giant library with all the books thrown on the floor. It's not very organized.

There are three kinds of connections to the Internet:

- Via an online service

- Dial-up

- SLIP/PPP

The first type of connection is provided by a commercial online service such as America Online or CompuServe. As this is being written, these services offer limited access to the Internet and no access to the World Wide Web.

That's changing, though. The major services are introducing browsers that look very much like the powerful Mosaic and Netscape. You'll be able to use them directly from your provider, without any kind of special connection. The first of these to become operational is offered by Prodigy, and it's pretty good. It might even be a reason for you to try Prodigy, even if it doesn't have other features that appeal to you.

The second type of connection is called a *dial-up* connection. You get a dial-up account from an Internet service provider. Using that account, you dial in and connect to your provider's computer and use that computer and software to connect to the Internet. Some providers of dial-up accounts offer their own form of graphical browser, but these are usually not considered as effective as a direct connection working with a browser such as Mosaic.

Finally, there's the kind of connection on which Mosaic and other graphical browsers can be used. It's called a SLIP/PPP account because of the kind of software you need to make the connection. A SLIP/PPP account is necessary for the most powerful connections to the Web.

What do we mean by powerful? To understand the difference between a dial-up account connection and a SLIP/PPP connection, imagine the stories you've read and pictures you've seen of nuclear power plants. Did you notice that sometimes the workers in the plant used a robot arm to move hazardous things around? This robot is like a dial-up account. The part that's in contact with the Internet is your provider's computer, and your computer is in contact with your provider's computer from the other side. SLIP/ PPP connections, on the other hand, are like handling the Internet yourself. In that power-plant analogy, it's like handling the material directly with your own hand.

One of the more exciting developments on the Internet and World Wide Web is the introduction of services that look and act very much like the powerful, direct-connect browsers—but they are available on dial-up accounts. Two such services are Netcom and Pipeline.

What Lies Ahead for the Internet

Things are changing very fast in the Internet world just now. You can expect commercial online services to provide you with more and easier ways to connect to the Internet. Those capabilities may be all you ever need. On the other hand, you can expect direct Internet connections to become easier to obtain and to use. And there will be more and more interesting resources available on the Internet as time goes on. Ultimately, you will have to make the decision about whether and how to hook up to the Internet based on *your* needs and the possibilities available to *you*. For right now, though, consider the following strategy.

How to Get Connected

Start by exploring the Internet using the connections available from your current online services. You'll be able to get an idea of what's out there, as well as whether you can use it. If it turns out that you want to try connecting to the Internet directly, start with a dial-up account. And it's probably best to start with one of the dial-up providers that offer a graphical browser, so you can check out the Internet.

For most folks, that will be plenty of Internet fun. If you find you need faster speed or more-sophisticated features, pick up one of the many books available on how to connect to the Internet. There you'll find good advice about how to choose a service provider and a software package. For right now, though, a connection through your commercial service or a graphical dial-up account should do the job for you.

Use the same strategy we've described for getting into the Internet/ WWW world to introduce yourself to parts of the online world; these techniques will work for the Internet as well. Find a friend who can show you what's possible. Get the friend to help you connect. Then move in small steps until you're comfortable with the basics. Finally, keep trying things and getting better.

CONCLUSION

Well, here we are, quite a ways from where we started. By now you've discovered the possibilities of the online world. You've explored and experienced. What's next? A lot of that depends on you. It depends on what you want.

One possibility is that you've achieved a sufficient level of knowledge and skills to meet your needs. It that's the case, then just keep doing those things that work for you. But don't stop exploring and poking around, because the online world is changing every day. There are always new features, new services and new things you can do.

Perhaps you want to move on to more sophisticated activities online. You may want to explore opportunities for doing business online, or maybe you want to hone your online research skills. Maybe you want to become a real "Internet surfer."

If any of these goals is your goal, then remember the basic strategies you've developed in this book. Find a friend. Watch. Try. Develop.

And always keep looking around for new developments. They're showing up all the time in the online world. Here are some future events to watch for:

► Expect it to become easier and easier to connect to the Internet and the World Wide Web through your commercial provider and through special services.

► Expect more and more of your friends and colleagues to be online. The growth rate for online services is positively astounding.

► You'll hear of some controversies about personal privacy, and security and crime online. It's bound to happen. As the demographics of the Net become more like the demographics of society as a whole, almost everything that's in the physical world will show up in the online world in some form. That includes crime and deviant behavior.

► Watch for changes that are unique to the digital, online world. We haven't figured out all the ramifications of copyrights and information sharing, for instance. The experts will get that done in the next few years.

► Finally, expect the online world to remain exciting and become increasingly productive for you and others. We're in the midst of a major evolution in how we live and do business. And you're right in the thick of it, so enjoy it.

Keep looking, keep exploring, keep growing. And share what you know and learn with others.

We'll see you online!

VI
GLOSSARY

BPS: Bits per second. A way to measure the speed of a modem or its ability to transmit data. The higher the number, the faster the modem will transmit. Often confused with baud rate, which measures the change in electrical signal during transmission of data. For most computer users the distinction is irrelevant. Call it bits per second or call it baud rate—the higher the number, the faster your modem.

Bulletin board: See computer bulletin board.

Chat room: The place on many commercial services where real-time conversation can happen.

Computer bulletin board (BBS): A system that allows people to use their computers to exchange messages, files and information. Many bulletin boards are small and have a special focus. Some, like CompuServe and America Online, are very large.

Cyberspace: An imaginary space where your online activity happens. It was originally defined and described by William Gibson in his novel, *Neuromancer*. This term is also used to refer to the online world in general.

Database: An ordered and searchable collection of information.

E-mail: Electronic mail lets users exchange messages over a computer network.

Emoticon: Symbols, made up of typed characters, that are used to show the emotion that would be conveyed in face-to-face communication by facial expression, voice tone, etc. One popular emoticon is the :-) used to indicate a smile. In fact, "smiley" is another term for emoticon.

FAQ file: The Frequently Asked Questions file. Most newsgroups and forums have a FAQ file that lays out the purpose of the forum or newsgroup and the rules that members should abide by.

Forum: Place on a major commercial service where people with like interests get together to discuss those interests by posting messages to each other. These are similar to newsgroups on the Usenet portion of the Internet. Forums usually have a message exchange board and a library of files related to the topic of the forum.

Freeware: Programs that you can use for free. Because they are copyrighted, though, you may not resell them for profit.

General purpose gateway: These services, America Online, Compu-Serve and Prodigy, provide their members with e-mail, shopping services, information and access to other services.

Graphical user interface (GUI): A way to work with a computer using menus and pictures as a way of entering commands. Macintosh and Windows computers use a GUI.

Hypertext: A way of displaying text in which key terms are linked to other terms or to a definition of the term. Most folks have some experience of hypertext while using the Help files included with their Mac or Windows programs.

The Internet: A globe-spanning computer communications network that links millions of smaller networks and their users. Services such as CompuServe and America Online use the Internet to exchange e-mail. The Internet started out as a government project to create a decentralized communications network that would not be vulnerable to enemy attack. For that reason, there is no central headquarters; no one owns or runs the Net. It's actually a system of protocols and agreements about how information should be exchanged.

Macro: A series of keystrokes or commands recorded and assigned to a single keystroke or command. They are used often in word processing and spreadsheet applications as a way to quickly do repetitive tasks. Many communications programs let you set up macros for the same reason.

Message board: The portion of a bulletin board or forum where members exchange messages.

Modem: A piece of equipment that translates the digital information patterns of a computer into analog patterns that can move over a phone line and vice versa.

Newsgroups: Groupings of messages based on topic or interest that are shared over Usenet. There are thousands of newsgroups on every topic imaginable. Most newsgroups have strict rules about what kinds of messages are appropriate.

Provider: A service that enables users to gain access to the Internet. Also called a service provider or Internet service provider.

Real-time: Refers to communication that happens when all parties are together online and exchanging information. Chat is a real-time communication; e-mail is not.

Script: A list of recorded instructions that tell your communications software how to perform a specific task or set of tasks. A script is more elaborate than a macro. The major online services all have scripts built into their proprietary software, to handle the sign-on process for you. Other communications programs often allow you to develop scripts for specific applications.

Shareware: Programs that you can try for free, but are legally obligated to pay for if you continue to use them. Many shareware programs are available in forum libraries online.

Special purpose gateways: Services that are set up to provide a single specific service (such as e-mail) or information from a single source (such as Dow Jones). They do not offer the range of services or information sources of general purpose gateways.

Terms of Service (TOS): The rules of a commercial online service such as CompuServe or America Online, setting out what you can and can't do on that service. Violation of Terms of Service may be grounds for canceling your account.

Usenet: Usenet is a system that uses the Internet to exchange messages in topic-related areas called newsgroups.